BATTLE
AT SEA

Text
Colin McIntyre

Photography
UPI/Bettmann
Keystone Collection
Peter Newark's Military Pictures

Design
Sally Strugnell

Commissioning Editor
Andrew Preston

Publishing Assistant
Edward Doling

Photo Research
Leora Kahn
Kenneth Johnston

Editorial
Jane Adams

Production
Ruth Arthur
David Proffit
Sally Connolly

Director of Production
Gerald Hughes

Director of Publishing
David Gibbon

CLB 2429
© 1990 Archive Publishing, a division of Colour Library Books Ltd.
Godalming, Surrey, England.
Printed and bound in Italy by New Interlitho.
All rights reserved.
ISBN 0 86283 809 6

WORLD WAR II

BATTLE AT SEA

COLIN McINTYRE

Bramley Books

The depth charge was the primary weapon used against submarines, in both the Atlantic and the Pacific. A large proportion of the 791 German U-boats lost in the War were either sunk by depth charges or brought to the surface by their explosion underwater.

CONTENTS

INTRODUCTION

Oceans cover five eighths of the surface of the earth. Conflicts between maritime countries, especially those involving island nations such as Great Britain and Japan, always lead to battles at sea as well as on land and in the air – at least in the years we are looking at here: 1939-1945.

Some of the most crucial and decisive battles of the Second World War were fought at sea. They would never completely settle the War one way or another, though the Battle of the Atlantic came close to doing so, and without the American victories in the Pacific, many won against considerable odds, the war with Japan might have ended in early 1945 with an unsatisfactory, negotiated peace.

This book looks at some of the decisive battles that were fought at sea between 3 September, 1939, and 10 August, 1945, and suggests why they are important, both in terms of naval history and in the part they played in an eventual Allied victory.

The aim is both to highlight and to illustrate, in layman's terms, just a few of the events that occurred. With hindsight, all of us feel we would make better admirals than those who were actually in charge at the time. We hardly need the advice of qualified naval strategists to decide how much better we would have done, if only we had been there or, for those who were there, if they had been in command and running the battles themselves.

Another aim of this book is to pay tribute both to those who took the decisions and to those who did the fighting. Finally it aims to suggest a few extra reasons why battles were never either as straightforward as one might think, or a simple matter of right or wrong choices.

The author is convinced that one major factor that too often gets played down or left out altogether is the role of the sea itself. It is easy to forget, when looking at neat little maps that trace the exact positions of ships in an engagement, all nicely calculated by historians after years of research, that very little of this was obvious to those on the spot at the time.

They had to operate within the full spectrum of that much-quoted phrase: 'the fog of war'. They almost certainly had to make decisions based on inadequate information and poor communications, in bad visibility, and with a hundred conflicting pressures on them.

Above all, they did so in the face of the sea itself. They did so aboard a pitching, heaving vessel, dodging through snow showers and rain squalls or, in the Pacific, amidst tropical storms and typhoons.

We should remember too the distances at which most battles were fought. The pictures in this book are inevitably after-the-battle close-ups, of sinking ships or rescued crews, with an occasional snapshot view taken from an attacking aircraft.

In many battles the enemy was often nothing more than a smudge on the horizon. In others, the aircraft-carrier battles that were to make this war unique, the surface forces never even sighted each other. For a six-foot man, the horizon is just over three miles; from the bridge of a ship at sea it is perhaps eleven or twelve miles. Think of a town twelve miles away from you and imagine firing naval guns that far

The 'safe and timely arrival' of a convoy (top right) - whether of merchantmen carrying vital supplies across the Atlantic or of troop transports delivering an Allied army to a beachhead - remained the key objective of all naval forces taking part in the battle at sea.

The worst fears about the power of the submarine were realised when U-29 sank the British aircraft carrier HMS *Courageous* (bottom right) in the first month of the war.

British seamen are helped aboard a U.S. Coast Guard cutter (left) after their ship was sunk by a German submarine. The incident was photographed at the height of the Battle of the Atlantic in 1943.

Communication was a problem throughout the Second World War. Methods used were often comparatively primitive, such as the use of semaphore during the landings in Sicily (left). Several battles might have ended differently if communications had been better and quicker, or standardised.

Anywhere the battle at sea was being fought - Sicily or Guadalcanal or Okinawa - there were survivors to be rescued from the sea. Two members of the Allied invasion forces are being rescued (right) after their landing craft struck a mine off Normandy on D-day, 6 June, 1944.

away. Picture too, what it was like to try and find even a fleet of battleships in a wide expanse of ocean, never mind trying to spot a submarine or a ditched aircrew.

Film and television documentaries condition us to the close-up. We expect to see a recognisable outline of some kind. Yet, with the exception of a few lucky submarine commanders, and possibly some unlucky ones as well, almost nobody on board ship ever saw an enemy warship outlined in the kind of silhouette that fills naval recognition manuals.

Even from aircraft, the problems of recognition were seldom much easier. In the search for the *Bismarck* in May 1941 an attack by sixteen aircraft from HMS *Ark Royal* was actually made on the British cruiser HMS *Sheffield*. Drastic avoiding action by the cruiser,

and the lucky failure of the magnetic torpedoes they were using, saved the *Sheffield*, but the story could have been quite different.

On 22 February, 1940, six German destroyers were making their way through minefields off the Dogger Bank to raid British shipping and fishing boats in the North Sea. A communication failure ensured that the *Luftwaffe* was not warned that some of the ships in the North Sea that night would be German. As a result, a single Heinkel 111 dive-bombed and sank two of the destroyers, the *Leberecht Maas* and the *Max Schulz*, and 578 German seamen died.

In darkness at sea it is not only impossible to identify friend from foe visually, but, when an attack comes, it is not always possible to be sure if it is from the air, from the surface or from under the sea.

'Combing' torpedoes is a term that appears frequently in naval narratives. It describes the kind of evasive action a ship's captain takes immediately torpedo tracks are spotted racing towards his ship at a speed of 30 or 40 knots.

Again, think of a parallel situation on land. Imagine the kind of split-second decision you would have to take as a car bomb hurtled towards you at 30 m.p.h. while you were travelling at about the same speed at the wheel of a huge truck, with a slow and limited turning circle.

Recognising torpedoes is often made to sound easy. However, in storm-tossed seas, and with every sign of turbulence or phosphoresence suspect, it is a brave man who, tired and cold at the end of a four-hour watch, is sure that what he is seeing is the real thing, and not just a dolphin, a sudden wave break or crosscurrent.

For most men at sea, and certainly for all but a handful of merchant seamen, the first torpedo they saw could also well have been their last. Even trained naval lookouts and ship's officers with naval reserve training would probably only have seen a maximum of half a dozen practice torpedoes, before war made them common.

Keeping watch myself, during a brief three weeks on an Atlantic convoy, I can testify to the near impossibility of an amateur being sure of what he saw. Even by day, identifying other ships or escort vessels in the convoy was no easy task. Deciding which ships are steaming by in a blacked-out night is best left to professionals.

Nothing in this book is meant to glorify war. It is intended as a dispassionate account of what happened, or what appears to have happened, during the battles at sea between 1939 and 1945.

I have done my best not to be partisan and to write out or ignore the bias present in even the best writing of the naval historians I have consulted. This is sometimes hardest to do when using pictures that were issued at the time. Some of the propaganda captions that came

The submarine and the aircraft carrier emerged from World War II as the most likely craft to survive the changing conditions of war at sea. At 14,000 tons and carrying 84 planes, the USS *Ranger* (left) was one of the smallest aircraft carriers in the U.S. Navy, but she proved very effective.

with them make one ashamed, until one remembers what the War was about and the untold miseries that an Allied defeat would have brought to half the world.

Finally, this book is a chance to salute the brave men on all sides who fought, and died, in the battle at sea. It is coupled with a reminder about the one element that we cannot ignore in any account of naval warfare – the sea itself.

BATTLE OF THE RIVER PLATE

Right: the *Admiral Graf Spee* is launched, to a forest of Nazi salutes, at Wilhelmshaven on 30 June, 1934. She was actually completed eighteen months later, in January 1936, in time to take part in cruises through Spanish waters during the Civil War, in which Germany supported General Franco against the Republican government.

Before the Second World War began, Germany sent out two of her three pocket battleships to act as raiders: the *Deutschland* to the North Atlantic and the *Admiral Graf Spee* to the South Atlantic.

Slipping out of Wilhelmshafen on 21 August, 1939, the *Graf Spee*, followed three days later by the *Deutschland*, sailed far north beyond the Faeroes. Neither ship was spotted either by the Royal Navy or by aircraft of RAF Coastal Command.

Hitler hoped that after his defeat of Poland, Britain and France would accept a negotiated peace. So for the first three weeks of war the two raiders were told not to attack any merchantmen.

Freed from this restriction on 26 September, 1939, the *Graf Spee* sank the 5,000-ton British steamer *Clement* off Pernambuco in Brazil, and the *Deutschland* sank the 5,000-ton *British Stonegate*.

Although the *Admiral Graf Spee*, under Captain Hans Langsdorff, went on to a very successful raiding career, the *Deutschland* did not. She next captured the U.S. merchantman *City of Flint* and then sank a Norwegian ship. Two neutral vessels out of three was extremely embarrassing, so she was ordered home, and her name was later changed to *Lutzow*. Hitler felt that, should she be sunk, the loss of a ship called the *Deutschland* would be too great a propaganda triumph for the enemy.

The *Admiral Graf Spee* was a fine ship. Supposedly restricted by naval treaties to 10,000 tons, she was in fact well over 12,000. Her main armament of six 11-inch guns, and a secondary armament of eight 6-inch guns, made her a powerful enemy for any British cruisers to tackle. Add thick armour plating and a speed of 26 knots and she was more than a match for any British ships about.

Her next successes as a raider were against

Left: circled and arrowed is some of the damage suffered at waterline level by the *Admiral Graf Spee*. The British argued that, as the pocket battleship had steamed some 300 miles since breaking off the battle, she could hardly claim to be unseaworthy, for which repairs would be legitimate. The Germans wanted the Uruguayans to allow them to restore her to full battleworthiness.

The *Admiral Graf Spee* in Montevideo Harbour (top right), which she entered after losing the Battle of the River Plate in order to effect the necessary repairs to enable her to face her British adversaries again. A fierce diplomatic battle took place about how long she was entitled to stay in this neutral port.

The *Admiral Graf Spee* (bottom right) was built with complete disregard for the applicable naval treaty limit of 10,000 tons. She was well over 12,000 tons, nearer 16,000 tons when fully loaded. Her six 11-inch guns and a secondary armament of eight 5.9-inch guns, together with heavy armour plating, made her a true pocket battleship.

ships using the sea route from Capetown, at the southernmost tip of South Africa, en route to Britain. In fairly quick succession she accounted for four more British merchant ships, *Newton Beech*, *Ashlea*, *Huntsman* and *Trevanion*, before deciding to make for the Indian Ocean.

Here she was less successful, sinking only the small tanker *Africa Shell* in the Mozambique Channel between the African mainland and the French island of Madagascar. She returned to the Atlantic again.

By then she was fulfilling another role in addition to sinking merchantmen. Simply by existing she tied up a large number of British warships, needed elsewhere, searching for her.

As well as the main British South Atlantic squadron of two 8-inch gun cruisers and two 6-inch gun cruisers under Commodore Henry Harwood RN (Force 'G'), there was another force of cruisers based on Capetown (Force 'H'), and much stronger forces further north, including several battleships and aircraft carriers.

A few days later, the *Admiral Graf Spee* sank two more British ships, but one of them, the 10,000 ton *Doric Star* managed to get off an R-R-R 'Raider Report' before she was sunk.

Commodore Harwood commanding Force 'G' then had to guess at Captain Langsdorff's intentions. Would the *Graf Spee* head north and homewards, or would she continue raiding. If so, would she attack the rich shipping traffic off Rio de Janeiro in Brazil, or that in the River Plate estuary between Argentina and Uruguay? Furthermore, would she raid the Falkland Islands, where the German Admiral after whom the ship was named had been defeated in World War I?

Harwood decided that the River Plate was the most likely objective. He ordered three of his cruisers – the 8-inch gun HMS *Exeter*, under Captain Frederick Bell, and the two smaller 6-inch gun cruisers: his flagship HMS *Ajax*, under Captain C.H.L. Woodhouse, and the New Zealand ship HMNZS *Achilles*, under Captain

Left: a closer view of damage to the *Admiral Graf Spee*, showing where British shellfire penetrated the hull near the waterline. Not all the black marks are actual holes, however; some are simply scars from shell splinters. In all, the *Admiral Graf Spee* was hit by three 8-inch shells from HMS *Exeter* and seventeen 6-inch shells from the two other cruisers. Only one pierced her armoured decks. Thirty-six of her crew were killed and sixty injured.

A sad end to any ship – the *Admiral Graf Spee*, after leaving Montevideo, sailed into the roads outside the harbour and was scuttled and blown up (right) by the skeleton crew that had remained on board. The rest had been taken off by the supply ship *Tacoma* and ferried across the River Plate to Buenos Aires.

Edward Parry – to rendezvous 150 miles east of the River Plate on 12 December, 1939. His other 8-inch gun cruiser, HMS *Cumberland,* was being refitted in the Falkland Islands, and could stay there and defend the islands if necessary.

Next day, shortly after 0600 hours, smoke was sighted and at 0614 HMS *Exeter* reported: 'I think it is a pocket battleship'. Indeed it was. The sea was calm, with a slight swell. As dawn broke, visibility was good. It was summer in the southern hemisphere.

Captain Langsdorff seems to have decided on his tactics beforehand. These were to close with any pursuing or shadowing cruiser, and rely on his heavier guns and superior armour to stop the enemy in their tracks. He turned towards the British force, and brought both his forward turrets to bear on HMS *Exeter*.

At 0618 hours the *Graf Spee* opened fire. *Exeter* replied at 0620, *Ajax* at 0621, and *Achilles* at 0623. The range was just short of eleven miles. The first proper naval battle of the Second World War had begun.

What Captain Langsdorff does not seem to have anticipated is that Commodore Harwood might deploy his ships not as a combined force, but as two separate forces. The British cruisers were faster, and could engage the *Graf Spee* from different directions. They were also able to spot the fall of shells from different angles, and thus positioned, help each other to be more accurate.

The *Graf Spee* soon had HMS *Exeter* within range. One shell burst amidships killing the ship's starboard torpedo crew and wrecking both her aircraft; a more direct hit put 'B' turret out of action and showered those on the bridge with shell splinters. Captain Bell was among the wounded.

The *Graf Spee* herself was hit by a shell from the *Exeter*, which damaged her control tower. More worrying at this stage, was the proximity of the two 6-inch gun cruisers, HMS *Ajax* and HMNZS *Achilles*. Captain Langsdorff had to turn his main guns away from HMS *Exeter*, and use them against his two terrier-like attackers, 13,000 yards away. Next, he had to alter course to avoid torpedoes fired by the *Exeter*.

Langsdorff changed direction again, and laid smoke. He then redirected his fire towards HMS *Exeter*, scoring further hits. He put another turret out of action and caused a fire amidships.

15

Yet he did not go in for the kill, even though HMS *Exeter* had only one turret working by this stage. Shells from the *Ajax* and the *Achilles*, while not penetrating the *Graf Spee*'s main armour, were wrecking her superstructure and causing casualties. Captain Langsdorff apparently decided to get away from his antagonists, now less than five miles distant, and fight the battle at the longer range more suited to his bigger guns.

This decision probably marked the moment when the Germans lost their will to win and their belief in victory, and sought escape to the west. It was not much more than an hour since the battle had begun, but HMS *Exeter* was also ready to break off battle. Her last turret was out of action, she was listing and had taken water aboard, sixty-one of her crew were dead and another twenty were wounded.

The battle, however, was not yet over. Aboard the *Ajax*, Commodore Harwood saw no reason to let the *Graf Spee* choose the range at which the battle would be fought. Using their superior speed, he took his two cruisers in closer. Although HMS *Ajax* had been hit and had had two turrets put out of action, she too had hit the pocket battleship and started a fire aboard her.

HMNZS *Achilles* then fired four torpedoes, and so in return did the *Graf Spee*, but all were avoided. The pursuit continued until Harwood received a report that ammunition was running low aboard the *Ajax* and, he presumed, probably also aboard the *Achilles*. It wasn't, but the report was enough to decide him to

return to the traditional cruiser-shadowing role, some fifteen miles from his large adversary.

The *Admiral Graf Spee* needed to seek repairs. She had used a good proportion of her ammunition, had a nasty six-foot hole in her bows, and was in no condition to head into a wintery North Atlantic, where hostile heavy forces were searching for her. Although only one British shell had penetrated her armour, much of her superstructure was wrecked. All the sixty-two captured British Merchant Navy officers and men aboard were safely battened down. Thirty-six of her crew were dead; sixty were wounded, six seriously.

The *Ajax* and the *Achilles* continued to shadow the *Graf Spee* for the rest of the day. Whenever either of the British cruisers approached too closely, Langsdorff fired a salvo or two. This didn't stop them approaching. When it became clear that the German ship was heading for the Uruguayan capital of Montevideo, Commodore Harwood ordered the *Achilles* to keep following. His own ship, the *Ajax*, was positioned to the south, in case the German ship doubled back.

As it got dark, the *Achilles* twice went in closer, provoking further salvoes. Nevertheless, by midnight, the *Graf Spee* had entered Montevideo roads and dropped anchor. The Battle of the River Plate was over.

The next battle was a diplomatic one. Langsdorff wanted to spend fifteen days making his ship sea- and battleworthy. However, the Hague Convention allows a warship to stay in a neutral port for only twenty-

HMNZS *Achilles*, together with another 6-inch gun cruiser HMS *Ajax* and the 8-inch gun cruiser HMS *Exeter*, drove the *Admiral Graf Spee* into Montevideo. The *Achilles* is entering Montevideo (left) after the German pocket battleship had been scuttled.

Cheerful crew members point out battle scars on the funnel of HMS *Exeter* (right) on her triumphant return to Britain after the Battle of the River Plate. The 8-inch gun cruiser suffered heavily at the guns of the *Admiral Graf Spee*. Sixty-one of her crew were killed and twenty were injured. The two smaller British cruisers escaped with much less damage and a combined total of only eleven dead.

four hours. An exception applies if she needs repairs to become seaworthy. The British Minister to Uruguay, Eugene Millington-Drake, pointed out that, as the *Graf Spee* had steamed some 300 miles since the battle had been broken off, she could hardly be considered unseaworthy and should be made to leave next day.

The Uruguayans announced that they would inspect the ship and declare how long she needed for repairs. Suddenly the British attitude was reversed: Commodore Harwood had decided he wanted more reinforcements himself, besides HMS *Cumberland* which had steamed up from the Falklands.

It was then, that clever use of rumour was made. Reports were circulated in Montevideo that a large British Fleet was already waiting outside Uruguayan territorial waters. The ships were said to include the battle cruiser HMS *Renown* and the aircraft carrier HMS *Ark Royal* – both still a good 1,000 miles away in reality.

British Minister Eugene Millington-Drake, inevitably known to all by the nickname 'Fluffington-Duck', went back to the Uruguayans and pointed out that under the Hague Convention a belligerent warship was not permitted to leave port within twenty-four hours of the departure of a merchant vessel belonging to the other side. A British merchantman hastily left port, which meant the *Graf Spee* was not entitled to sail before the evening of 16 December, 1939.

These machinations were a delight to the newspaper world, providing a new lead to the *Graf Spee* story every twelve hours or so. It was all settled when the Uruguayans decreed a stay of seventy-two hours, and no more.

Captain Langsdorff consulted Berlin. He thought his ship's condition meant almost certain destruction by the forces he believed were ranged against him outside Montevideo. He also expressed doubt at having much chance of damaging his attackers. Should he accept internment in Uruguay, or destroy his ship? Hitler ruled against internment.

On 17 December, 1939, some 700 of the *Graf Spee*'s crew were taken aboard the German tanker *Tacoma*, and shortly after 6.00 p.m., with only a skeleton crew aboard, the German pocket battleship weighed anchor.

Watched by crowds, and with radio reporters giving a running commentary on the scene, the *Admiral Graf Spee* slowly pulled out of the harbour. Four miles out she stopped and

dropped anchor. Captain Langsdorff and the skeleton crew left. Then at 8.00 p.m. there was a series of six loud explosions aboard. She blew up and caught fire, and was soon nothing but a blazing hulk. The *Graf Spee* had been scuttled rather than have to fight again.

The crew of the *Graf Spee* were taken to Buenos Aires, the Argentine capital on the other side of the River Plate estuary. They would be seen for a few weeks, sad and forlorn figures, being entertained in the homes of members of the German community in Argentina, and still in uniform. Eventually they would be interned, though most of the officers and a few of the more resolute of the men soon escaped and made their way back to Germany. For the bulk of them, however, the war was over. Some settled in Argentina, the rest would be repatriated in 1946.

Captain Langsdorff was not interned. He wrote farewell letters to his wife and family, and to the German Ambassador, and then shot himself. His body was found lying on a German naval ensign in the hotel bedroom he had

Left: Captain Hans Langsdorff, commander of the German pocket battleship *Admiral Graf Spee*, attending the funeral in Montevideo of the thirty-six members of his crew killed in the Battle of the River Plate. Aged forty-five, he committed suicide in Buenos Aires on 19 December, 1939, six days after the battle.

Right: Nazi salutes figure prominently at Captain Hans Langsdorff's funeral in Buenos Aires. He was never considered a fanatical Nazi, and is said to have chosen to die on a German naval flag, which did not carry the swastika. Captain Pottinger, of the British merchantman SS *Ashlea*, one of the sixty-two captured British seamen who were aboard the *Admiral Graf Spee* throughout the battle and all of whom were unhurt, represented them at the funeral.

been allotted within the naval area in the port of Buenos Aires.

The Battle of the River Plate, and the events surrounding it, belong almost to another age – a bygone age of chivalry, of a comradeship of the sea and of a restraint far removed from 'Total War'. In ten weeks of raiding, Captain Langsdorff had sunk nine British merchant ships, totalling about 50,000 tons, without causing a single loss of life. The captured British officers and seamen aboard the *Graf Spee* all escaped the battle unscathed. Captain Pottinger of the SS *Ashlea* would represent them all at Langsdorff's funeral.

It was a battle that would prove untypical of the majority during the War: fought in good weather, with aircraft playing only a very minor spotting role. Three smaller and less heavily-armoured British cruisers had fought an almost classic battle and defeated one of Admiral Raeder's most prized ships.

The final episode of the *Graf Spee* saga belongs equally to that bygone era. The captain of the *Altmark*, the pocket battleship's supply ship, disregarded orders to land the 299 captive British seamen at a neutral port, and made a run for Germany. Intercepted in Norwegian waters, he denied that he had any prisoners aboard.

British destroyers cornered the *Altmark* in Josing Fiord, and HMS *Cossack*, under Captain P.L. Vian, prepared to board her. The *Altmark* turned on searchlights to blind those on the destroyer's bridge and did her best to ram HMS *Cossack*. The *Cossack*'s boarding party leapt onto the decks of the *Altmark*, and after a short fierce fight, in which six *Graf Spee* guards were killed, it was all over.

The boarding party opened the hatches of the *Altmark* and asked: 'Any British down there?'. There was an answering roar, and then the famous words were shouted back: 'Come on up, the Navy's here.'

It would be a long time before the British again won such a heartening victory as the Battle of the River Plate; or enjoyed such a colourful triumph as the rescue of the *Altmark*'s prisoners.

CONVOY

The battle at sea in the Second World War soon involved every ship which left harbour, not just those of the belligerent nations. Both Britain *and* Germany declared a blockade and issued warnings that they would intercept all ships making for one of their enemy's ports.

In the early days this meant British naval vessels, generally armed merchant cruisers, stopping neutral vessels and searching them for contraband destined for the German war effort. German U-boats on the surface stopped ships, and sank them by gunfire, or, if they were neutrals, let them sail on. Such niceties would soon be forgotten.

As merchantmen were given defensive guns, and trained to send out attack reports, U-boats began to torpedo all ships in enemy waters on sight. Indeed, within ten hours of war being declared between Britain and Germany, U-30, already in position 250 miles out in the Atlantic, torpedoed the 13,800 ton British liner *Athenia*. Along with eighteen of her crew, 112 passengers died, twenty-eight of them Americans. The *Athenia* was not in convoy, but rather an outward-bound independent, travelling at full speed and zigzagging furiously.

German attacks directed against merchant shipping in the European theatre of war lasted for very nearly six years. Some 5,000 merchant ships would be sunk, 2,828 of them by submarines. The total tonnage lost was over twenty-one million, half of it British.

The *Athenia*, sunk on 3 September, 1939, was the first U-boat victim. The Canadian steamer *Avondale Park* would have the dubious distinction of being the last vessel to be sunk in European waters in the Second World War. She was torpedoed in the Firth of Forth on 7 May, 1945, by U.2336, whose captain had apparently not heard the ceasefire orders issued after the German Army had surrendered.

The Allies had to win this continuing battle if they were going to win the war. Britain had to be fed, and also supplied with the equipment and war materials without which she would be overrun by the German Army, as France and the rest of the continent of Europe had been.

The first measure taken was a defensive one; it was to reintroduce the convoy system which had been used in World War I. Apart from troop convoys carrying the British Expeditionary Force across the Channel, convoys had not been used until late 1917. It was only then that they were more or less imposed on a reluctant British Admiralty by Prime Minister Lloyd George.

In World War I, regular navy men used just about every argument they could think of against convoys. They said that merchant captains could never manage the discipline required to sail together in large groups of ships, and would be unable to keep station as the Royal Navy did. Naval practice at the time was seen almost entirely in terms of large-scale engagements between battle fleets. These depended for their success on carefully developed manoeuvres and tactics, practised and synchronised in fleet exercises worked out over many years.

Naval men objected to detaching valuable

Calm seas, a rare event, mean that an Atlantic convoy can keep station. The picture shows the 'squareness' of a typical convoy, comprising anything up to a dozen or more columns, each only a few ships deep. Two warships of the close escort, one out in front and the other out to the side can also be seen.

An almost idyllic convoy scene shows the ships closed up at dusk, under the watchful eye of the U.S. Coast Guard cutter from which the photograph was taken.

destroyers from protecting the battleships, which might be needed at any moment to confront those of the German Navy. They also argued that bringing ships together in convoy merely provided U-boats and raiders with a better target.

It was tragic to hear almost the same arguments resurfacing in 1939. The Royal Navy had managed to convince itself that this war would also consist of large-scale engagements between surface ships as the only way to decide who ruled the waves.

If proof were needed of the value of convoys, this came in the first four months of the War. Of the 106 merchant ships sunk in this period, only four were lost from escorted convoys. All the rest were sailing independently or were stragglers who dropped out of a convoy with engine trouble or proved incapable of keeping up the speed they had promised.

Yet in many ways convoys were inefficient. Departure of ships had to be delayed until the right numbers for a convoy had assembled. A convoy's top speed would always be, in that classic phrase, 'the speed of the slowest ship in the convoy'. Their common route did make it easier for an enemy to find them, and prepare the kind of 'wolf-pack' ambushes that Admiral Donitz had forecast before the War. In addition, when a convoy reached its destination it created a bottleneck as all the ships needed unloading at the same time. Finally, travelling in convoy added at least one third more to the duration of the passage that most of the ships were designed for.

The wide range of ships to be convoyed is hard to picture today. There were old tramp steamers and fast refrigerated meat carriers, there were LSTs (Landing Ships, Tanks) never intended for Atlantic crossings and oil tankers of every shape and size. Later there were mass-produced Liberty ships straight off the assembly line, together with ships that had started their careers long before World War I.

The ships were also of every nationality, right from the earliest days of the War. By mid-1940, when Europe had been overrun, merchant ships of most of the occupied countries were at sea in the Allied cause. There were also chartered neutrals, Panama-registered vessels, and ships from Iceland, which Britain occupied on 10 May, 1940, after Hitler's invasion of Denmark, and which U.S. marines would take over in 1941.

We shall return to convoys again and again in future chapters, because the battle between Germany's U-boats and the Allied navies and air forces was not only the longest battle of World War II, but in many ways the most important.

Without going into great detail, some understanding of convoy procedure is needed to follow the tragic destruction of PQ17 and the course of the Battle of the Atlantic. The man in charge of the merchant ships was the convoy commodore. Generally this position was held by a retired regular naval officer or a senior merchant captain who was a member of the Naval Reserve. Several retired admirals also served as convoy commodores, nominally stepping down in rank to do so.

The commodore, however senior, took his orders from the SOE (senior officer, escort), however junior. The escort ideally consisted of two sections, the close escort, who were supposed to stay with their merchant ships whatever happened, and a supporting escort, who were seen, perhaps wrongly, as an offensive force, to hunt down submarines. This ideal was seldom achieved and many escorts were composed of whatever ragbag collection of destroyers, corvettes, tugs and minesweepers were available at the time.

As the Atlantic battle developed and the U-boat 'packs' attacked as an organised naval force, the Allies went in for 'hunter-killer' groups. These were not supporting escorts so much as a strike force designed to operate alongside, but not as part of, a convoy.

There would be a good deal of argument about how best to protect a convoy. However much it went against the grain, it was probably better for the escorts to stay with their charges, and not to try and carry the war to the enemy. There were too many cases of escorts charging after a U-boat contact, while other submarines moved in for a kill on the real target, the merchantmen. Sinking a U-boat was simply a bonus, while preventing a U-boat from launching an attack was in itself sufficient justification for the work of an escort.

Their purpose, after all, was to see that the convoying ships got to their destination safely and on time. Until the Germans developed tactics that allowed them to challenge convoys directly, a large proportion of the ships they sank were vessels travelling alone, or stragglers that had become detached from their protecting escorts.

Convoys were given letters and numbers, the letters denoting the route they were following, and the numbers denoting their historical position in the chain. Thus, ONS169 was an outward-bound slow convoy from the U.K. to North America in February-March 1943. Likewise, the letters KX indicated a military convoy from the U.K. to North Africa sailing for Operation Torch in October 1942. A feature of convoys that is not always appreciated is the pattern in which the ships were generally arranged. Somehow one tends to think of them in terms of a school crocodile, pairs of infants in a long file, being shepherded by a few flanking teachers, with a junior teacher or assistant bringing up the rear.

Convoys were much squarer than that. Depending on the number of ships, they might sail together in a broad pattern of twelve or fourteen columns, each one six ships deep at the most. From the front you saw a dozen or more columns of ships coming at you, from the side a frieze of only four to six ships.

The convoy commodore nearly always led from the centre front. Depending on numbers, he would probably have a vice commodore who would take over if his ship were sunk, and perhaps a rear commodore to help control things from behind. These posts were simply appointments given to senior masters of merchant ships with experience of convoy work. Only the convoy commodore had a staff and probably extra signallers, and equipment, working for him.

Needless to say, most of the fears of the regular navy men about convoy discipline proved as ill-founded in the Second World War as they had in the First. Most of the masters and their merchant marine watchkeeping officers were as good at keeping station and dealing with the hazards of the sea as any destroyer captain. Indeed, the masters in particular probably had many more years seagoing experience than the young naval officers of the escorts. However, they remained civilians. Though they accepted the need for discipline and for 'doing it the navy way' while in the convoy, their primary responsibility was still to the ships and their owners. Many of the merchant navy skippers were independent-minded men, who had not reached their positions by accepting either every order or strategy decreed by modern fashion or the diktats of bureaucratic administrators directing their fate from afar.

There were also less experienced masters and, much more often, ill-trained and selfish crews, the price of recruiting according to the dictates of expediency.

A photograph taken in 1942, when the Atlantic battle against the U-boats was raging fiercely, gives a more realistic picture of Atlantic conditions, though the sea is still relatively calm. The swell does, however, illustrate that it was not easy to keep station at all times.

Top left: twin-mounted anti-aircraft machine guns on the stern of a British freighter. Most ships carried such weapons simply to deter enemy aircraft from attempting low-level attacks. There would probably also be a 4-inch anti-submarine gun. These weapons were generally handled by naval or army gunners carried aboard the merchant ships, but members of the crew were often also trained to use the guns, so that they too could play a part in helping to defend their ships when under attack.

The introduction of specially equipped rescue ships was a key factor in maintaining the morale of merchant seamen sailing in convoys and liable to U-boat attacks. The rescue ships sailed at the rear of a convoy and did their best to pick up survivors from torpedoed ships. In April 1942, the Canadian Navy picked up thirty-eight of the crew of this wrecked ship (bottom left).

Right: a freighter sailing in a heavy swell after a gale in the North Atlantic in April 1945, photographed from a following troop transport manned by the U.S. Coast Guard. Spotting a periscope, torpedo tracks or even a surfaced submarine from a rolling ship was a very difficult task.

The trans-Atlantic convoys, leaving from Nova Scotia, Newfoundland or, in later days, New York – or sailing from the United Kingdom for these places – completed the crossing in varying times. Depending on the weather, the routeing and the speed of the convoy, the average passage would be around seventeen days, compared with ten at most in peacetime.

Seventeen days bucking through heavy seas was not something to look forward to. Quite apart from the fog, mist and storms there was the ever-present threat of being torpedoed by a submarine, or even blasted by a surface-raiding battleship or a heavy cruiser.

It is also easy to forget the many ordinary marine hazards the seamen in these convoys had to contend with. Green seas swept aboard, lookouts and guns froze up, deck cargo shifted in the winter gales, and watch-keeping went on day after day with no break.

Within a year or so of the start of the War, German air power had virtually closed London, Britain's largest and most-used port. The Atlantic convoys were now all going to west coast ports: to Londonderry in Northern Ireland, to Greenock in Scotland, and, above all, to the large port of Liverpool in England. From these ports coastal convoys would travel round the beleaguered British Isles. Often, ships that had safely crossed the Atlantic would fall prey to German aircraft and submarines, and even to raiding E-boats, as they made their way in coastal waters.

Many convoy battles are extremely well-documented. This is particularly true of the passage across the Atlantic of three convoys in the crucial month of March 1943: SC122, HX229 and HX229A. Martin Middlebrook's book *Convoy* gives an extremely clear account of the running battles that took place, involving between thirty-eight and forty-four U-boats at various times. These included two U-boats acting as 'tankers', and several others that made no attacks.

Historian John Terraine, in his excellent account of the U-boat wars of 1916-1945, *Business in Great Waters,* was writing a dozen years later than Middlebrook. He analyses Middlebrook's book and finds most points still valid.

Terraine also stresses the importance of the weather; from the storms, snow, ice and fog to the actual collision with an iceberg that sank the tanker *Svend Foyn.* The *Svend Foyn* and two escorts, also damaged by weather, were the only casualties suffered by convoy HX229A. This was a fast and valuable convoy, and included thirteen fast tankers, eight large refrigerated ships and four cargo liners. It headed far to the north and was missed by the U-boats.

Convoy SC122 had got off to a bad start. After sailing from New York on 5 March, the convoy ran into a violent storm two days into the journey, which broke up the columns and left eleven ships missing. One was never seen again, and several others had to return to port with storm damage, all long before a single U-boat was encountered. By 14 March, both SC122 and HX229 were being hit by winds of up to Force 10 and were sailing in sea states of 7-8 ('very high' and 'precipitous' respectively). Although these conditions were almost as difficult for the U-boats , they caused several convoy ships to drop behind and become easy targets.

The full details of the battle are to be found in the books mentioned. Suffice to know that, in all, twenty-two Allied merchantmen were sunk. 360 seamen, with twelve passengers, lost their lives in the two convoys hit by the U-boats. Only one U-boat, U-384, was sunk, probably by a land-based Flying Fortress. The submarine was on her first patrol; there were no survivors.

Mussolini proclaimed the Mediterranean to be *Mare Nostrum*, Our Sea. The Royal Navy would ensure that it was anything but that.

The Mediterranean in World War II was the scene of fierce fighting and some desperate convoy battles, but more than anything else the battles there served as a pointer to things to come in the war at sea. For the first time it became clear that future sea warfare would depend as much on air power as on the big guns of the navies.

Until France surrendered in June 1940, the Mediterranean was dominated by the British and French navies. The British had bases in Gibraltar at the Mediterranean's Atlantic end, at Alexandria in Egypt, and on Malta in the centre. The French controlled the western Mediterranean from their North African bases at Oran, Mers-el-Kebir and Bizerta, and from the great French naval port of Toulon.

With the fall of France, and Italy's entry into the War, the situation changed radically, and would do so again more a year or so later when Hitler moved powerful German air groups southwards.

Sadly, the British Navy had the unenviable task of ensuring that Admiral Darlan's French naval forces did not fall into Axis hands. This led to British attacks on the ships of their former allies at Oran, Mers-el-Kebir, and around in west Africa, on Dakar. The distress aroused by these attacks would have an impact on the North African landings of Operation Torch two years later.

Apart from invading Albania in April 1940, Italy had sat on the fence while Germany smashed the British and French armies in France. Four days before the Germans entered Paris, Mussolini declared war on Hitler's side. In September 1940, Italian troops invaded Egypt and started the fighting in the Western Desert that would go on for nearly three years. In October 1940 Italian troops invaded Greece. The Mediterranean had become an active theatre of war.

The British naval commander in the Mediterranean, Admiral Andrew B. Cunningham, with a force of five battleships, two aircraft carriers and ten 6-inch gun cruisers, faced what seemed to be a formidable enemy. Italy's four battleships, seven 8-inch and fourteen 6-inch gun cruisers included some of the newest and fastest warships in the world. More importantly, they were backed by a strong air force, many of whose pilots had undergone combat service in the Spanish Civil War.

At that time, British aircraft carriers did not carry fighters to help defend their fleet, only reconnaisance planes and torpedo bombers. In the first few months of confrontation there were a number of engagements between British and Italian forces, but none of great significance. In the main, the Italians stayed in port and made only occasional sallies to protect their convoys to Libya.

The first important clash came on 9 July, 1940, when a British submarine reported that two Italian battleships, the *Conte di Cavour* and the *Guilio Cesare*, were supporting a convoy bound for Libya. Admiral Cunningham, with three battleships, an aircraft carrier, five cruisers and seventeen destroyers headed to intercept.

Despite Italian air attacks, which damaged the British cruiser HMS *Gloucester*, and unsuccessful attempts by torpedo-carrying

Left: a Fairey Swordfish torpedo bomber takes off from HMS *Illustrious*. In November 1940, less than two dozen of these old-fashioned biplanes attacked the Italian fleet, which was anchored at Taranto in the heel of Italy. The battleship *Littorio* was sunk and two other battleships hit. It was an early lesson in the importance of air power which the Japanese did not fail to observe.

The Royal Air Force was used in a much more tactical way in the Western Desert than was the practice elsewhere at that stage in the War. Many of the lessons learned in North Africa about air support for the army would be applied in Europe after D-day. In early 1941, the RAF hit and set on fire the Italian cruiser *San Giorgio* (top right), leaving her settled on the bottom in Tobruk harbour.

Bottom right: British cruisers on convoy escort in the Mediterranean get up speed prior to facing an air attack. Air power would prove a key factor in many Mediterranean naval battles and in the British evacuations from Greece and Crete.

aircraft from HMS *Eagle* to slow the Italians down, the gunfight was soon over. The Italian heavy cruiser *Bolzano* was damaged, and a single fifteen-inch shell from Cunningham's flagship HMS *Warspite* hit the battleship *Giulio Cesare* at long range.

The Italian fleet departed behind a smoke screen and, although pursued to within twenty-five miles of the Italian coast, escaped.

Ten days later, five British destroyers encountered two Italian cruisers, and retired, closely pursued, in the direction of their supporting cruiser, the Australian 6-inch gun HMAS *Sydney*. The *Sydney* shattered and sank one of the pursuers, the *Bartolomeo Colleoni*, and seriously damaged the other, the *Giovanni delle Bande Nere*.

After these two clashes the Italians made no further attempts to get in the way of British operations for over two months. The British navy

The direction in which her guns are pointing, shows where the British cruiser (left) thinks the danger lies. She is prepared to face an air attack, whilst on convoy duty in the Mediterranean.

Right: a pom-pom gun crew, aboard a British destroyer, closed up and ready for action whilst on patrol in the Eastern Mediterranean, in May 1942.

The Mediterranean saw a good deal of underwater warfare, with submarines from all the belligerents attacking each other's convoys and warships. Top left: HMS *Barham* listing after being torpedoed on 25 November, 1941. The only British battleship to be sunk at sea by a U-boat during World War II, she blew up a few minutes later with the loss of 859 officers and men. Built in 1915, the twenty-five-year old vessel was hit at close range by torpedoes from U-331. A year later, U-331 was herself sunk in the Mediterranean by planes from HMS *Formidable*.

The end of the confrontation between the Italian and British navies came when Italy sued for peace, and an armistice was signed on 3 September, 1943. British sailors on HMS *Warspite* watch the arrival of a Littorio-class battleship in Malta (bottom left), where the Italian fleet had been ordered.

was kept busy escorting troops to Malta and flying in aircraft reinforcements, as well as bombarding the Libyan coast in support of the army.

Then, in November 1940, Cunningham decided to take the initiative. He launched an air attack on the Italian battle fleet in harbour at Taranto, its main base in the south of Italy.

Compared to later aircraft carrier attacks it was all on a pitiably small scale. Cunningham's force had been strengthened by the arrival of HMS *Illustrious* with her twelve fighters and twenty-two torpedo bombers and reconnaisance aircraft. On the other hand, HMS *Eagle* had been damaged by a fire in a hangar and could not take part. Five of the *Eagle*'s torpedo bombers and their crews transferred to the *Illustrious*.

Cunningham sailed from Egypt with four battleships, supporting cruisers and destroyers, and the *Illustrious*. On 11 November, 1940, two strike forces left the aircraft carrier roughly one hour apart, the first force consisting of twelve torpedo bombers, the second of nine.

The Italian fleet was taken by surprise. Despite anti-aircraft fire, the Fairey Swordfish made their approaches. With three torpedoes they sank the battleship *Littorio*, and then hit the 69 *Conte di Cavour* and the *Caio Duilio* with a single torpedo each. Half Italy's battleships had been put out of action, for the loss of two ancient biplanes and five torpedoes.

The Swordfish are supposed to have escaped destruction because nobody on the ground or in the ships believed that any aircraft would fly so slowly. With an absolute maximum speed of 160 m.p.h. the anti-aircraft gunners were all aiming hopelessly far in front.

Four and a half months later Admiral Cunningham would win the biggest naval battle of the War up to that point. It was fought off Cape Matapan in Greece, in that part of the Ionian Sea to the west of a line drawn between the Greek mainland and the island of Crete. Although the result was not as decisive as it might have been, its influence went beyond the statistics for ships sunk or damaged.

Italy's Eastern Fleet set out on a foray on 27 March, 1941, to attack British troop transports and supply ships going to Greece. Their secondary aim was to attack the British naval base established at Suda Bay in Crete. They relied on land-based aircraft for their protection, but failed to carry out some very necessary air

reconnaissance.

The British, on the other hand, thanks to radio intelligence and aircraft reports, knew exactly what was happening. Cunningham, flying his flag in HMS *Warspite* under Captain D.B. Fisher, left Alexandria and headed straight towards the Italians. By then the enemy had split their forces, one group going towards the north of Crete, the other sailing south of Crete to find the convoys. The battleship *Vittorio Veneto*, under Captain Sparzani and flying the flag of Vice-Admiral Iachino, was in the rear, in support of both squadrons.

All day and through the night the Italian and British fleets steamed on a collision course. At 0745 hours on 28 March, 1941, the British light cruiser HMS *Orion*, scouting ahead of Cunningham's force, encountered the *Vittorio Veneto*, which opened fire on her. The Italian battleship pursued the *Orion* – straight towards the British battleships *Warspite*, *Valiant* and *Barham*.

It was then that an air strike from the aircraft carrier HMS *Formidable*, some one hundred miles behind the battle fleet, once again proved what air power was for. In three attacks, at 11.30 a.m., 3.30 p.m. and dusk, its torpedo bombers successfully attacked the *Vittorio Veneto* and one of the groups of Italian cruisers.

The *Vittorio Veneto* having narrowly escaped several times and only too aware by now of the presence of three British battleships, turned away after the first air attack. She was hit by HMS *Formidable*'s second strike, a torpedo hitting her above her port propellor. She shipped a lot of water, but was able to keep going. The Italian cruiser *Pola* was not so lucky, being badly damaged in the third strike. With her steering gone she was soon stopped and vulnerable.

The climax of this battle came at about 10.00 p.m. The British fleet descended upon the stricken *Pola*, and two other Italian heavy cruisers and four destroyers that had returned to help her. The British took these ships by surprise, their guns still trained fore and aft, and most of the crews abed.

The destroyer HMS *Greyhound* used her searchlight to illuminate the enemy whilst HMS *Warspite*, at a range of about 4,000 yards, wrecked the 8-inch gun *Fiume*. The same fate met the *Zara* and two Italian destroyers, the *Alfieri* and the *Carducci*. British destroyers later used torpedoes to finish off all three cruisers.

At one stage HMS *Jervis* went alongside the *Pola* and took off twenty-two Italian officers and 236 men who were still on board. There was even some thought of trying to tow the cruiser back to Alexandria as a prize of war, but the danger from Axis aircraft was too great.

Nevertheless it was a singular victory. The British picked up some 1,000 Italian seamen as prisoners before they were forced to leave their rescue operations by the advent of dawn, and the threat of land-based air attacks.

They wirelessed the position of the remaining survivors, and more would be picked up by an Italian hospital ship and other vessels, but Italian losses were still high at around 3,000. The British lost two aircraft, but not a single man aboard their warships.

The victory had been an incomplete one, however, for the damaged *Vittorio Veneto*, which at first was even thought to have sunk, managed to reach her home base. Incredibly, when eight British destroyers led by HMS *Jervis*, under Captain Philip Mack, were sent after her, they missed her. The *Vittorio Veneto* had worked up a speed of 20 knots – 5 knots faster than her estimated maximum. The destroyers missed the damaged battleship by thirty miles.

There were several cases of mistaken identity during that confused night of battle. Separate squadrons sailed past in the darkness without identifying each other. At one stage the Italian cruisers returning to support the *Pola* were thought to be the British cruisers, and ignored. At another, both the British cruisers and destroyers spotted a red rocket signal, but each thought the other force was dealing with it.

Finally, there was a controversial signal given by Admiral Cunningham – the kind of signal best interpreted with hindsight in naval memoirs. In the midst of a fierce melee between destroyers, in which everyone was firing torpedoes, Cunningham signalled: 'All ships not engaged in sinking the enemy steer to the northeastward.' He meant it to refer only to those destroyers milling around the British battleships. It was not intended for the eight destroyers pursuing the *Vittorio Veneto*, which Cunningham thought were engaged in action with the enemy. They were not, and obediently steered northeast.

Even if the Battle of Cape Matapan was not as decisive as Cunningham and all naval strategists would have liked it to be, it *was* influential. Thereafter the Italian fleet would never again attempt to intervene in this same way. Had they done so, the British evacuations from both Greece and Crete might have been even more hard-pressed than they actually were.

Nor did the Italians attempt any major sorties as a battle fleet against the Malta convoys, which they might well have done had they been successful at Cape Matapan. Malta was able to hold out for three years against constant attacks. Despite being so close to Sicily and the heel of Italy, she never contemplated surrender. Malta fully earned the George Cross which King George VI awarded to the island and its people.

Nine months later the Axis powers had their revenge when German U-boat U-331 sank the battleship HMS *Barham*. Her captain and 861 of her crew were lost, but 450 were saved. She was to be the only Allied battleship sunk at sea in European waters by a submarine, although HMS *Royal Oak* had, of course, been sunk in 1939 while at anchor in the supposedly safe harbour of Scapa Flow in Scotland's Orkney Isles.

Further revenge followed a month later, on the night of 18 December, 1941. Three manned 'chariots' from the Italian submarine *Scire* penetrated Alexandria harbour and fixed explosive charges to the battleships *Queen Elizabeth* and *Valiant*.

Nonetheless, the man who dominated sea warfare in the Mediterranean in those early years of the War was undoubtedly Admiral A.B. Cunningham. He would go on to become an admiral of the fleet and would ultimately be ennobled as Viscount Cunningham of Hyndhope.

In a scene reminiscent of the surrender of the German High Seas Fleet at Scapa Flow in 1919, the Italian Navy lies off Malta following the armistice signed in September 1943. Plans to incorporate the Italian battle squadron into the British Fleet going to the Pacific were abandoned when it proved impossible to ensure a supply of spares and equipment for them from Allied sources.

SINKING THE BISMARCK

Germany's mightiest battleship, the *Bismarck*, was launched on 14 February, 1939, in Hamburg. She was christened by the Countess Dorothy von Lowenfeld, a granddaughter of the Iron Chancellor, Prince Otto Eduard Leopold von Bismarck (1815-1895), after whom the battleship was named.

In May 1941 a running battle in the North Atlantic resulted in the loss of HMS *Hood* and the sinking of Germany's mightiest battleship, the *Bismarck*. It was to be one of the last encounters of its kind.

Between them, both sides made almost every mistake in the book; victory was nevertheless achieved because at the same time the Royal Navy also obeyed most of the rules for success in war. If that sounds contradictory, that is the way of battle at sea.

After the loss of the *Admiral Graf Spee* in the River Plate in December 1939, Hitler was fairly cautious with his use of warships. The *Admiral Scheer* was out raiding for nearly six months in the winter of 1940-1941. She sank 100,000 tons of shipping and the armed merchant cruiser HMS *Jervis Bay*, whilst the latter was protecting her convoy.

The heavy cruiser *Admiral Hipper* made two raids in late 1940 and early 1941, one more successful than the other. The battleships *Scharnhorst* and *Gneisenau* were also out in early 1941, under Admiral Lutjens. Though they were deterred by battleships from attacking two big convoys, they still sank over 100,000 tons of shipping.

As a reward, Admiral Lutjens was appointed to command Hitler's next major naval sortie, flying his flag in the *Bismarck*, under Captain Lindemann. The cruiser *Prinz Eugen*, under Captain Brinkmann, was to provide support. Plans to involve the *Scharnhorst* and the *Gneisenau* were shelved; they had both suffered RAF bomb damage in Brest.

The *Bismarck* and the *Prinz Eugen* were in the Baltic, facing a difficult passage to the North Sea and the Atlantic. They had to pass through the narrow Kattegat between Denmark and Sweden and the almost equally narrow Skaggerak between Denmark and Norway.

They were spotted by a Swedish warship. Learning of this, the British naval attaché in Stockholm, alerted the Admiralty in London. Strike one to intelligence. An RAF Coastal Command attempt to bomb them while they lay in a Norwegian fjord failed.

The commander in chief of the British Home Fleet, Admiral Tovey, began moving ships into place as soon as he knew there was a possibility that the *Bismarck* might come out. He already had a force of cruisers patrolling the wide stretch between Iceland and the Faeroes. There was also a regular cruiser patrol in the narrower passage of the Denmark Strait between Iceland and Greenland – the route the *Bismarck* would choose.

In the Denmark Strait, the cruiser *Suffolk* was about to be relieved by another 8-inch gun cruiser, the *Norfolk*. Flying the flag of Rear-Admiral Wake-Walker, she would play a key role in the battle. Admiral Tovey despatched the battlecruiser HMS *Hood*, together with the battleship HMS *Prince of Wales*, to Iceland, to support the waiting and watching cruisers.

The decision to send the *Prince of Wales* was a brave one, for she was so new that contractors were still working on some of her 14-inch guns, and she had not completed her working-up period.

Tovey's main Home Fleet force at Scapa Flow included his own flagship, the battleship HMS *King George V*, under Captain Patterson; a dozen or so cruisers and destroyers; the battlecruiser HMS *Repulse* and an aircraft carrier, the HMS *Illustrious*, the latter two detached from convoy escort duties.

That important element in all battles in northern waters, bad weather, soon began to play its part. The two German ships had slipped out to sea while visibility was low, hence their absence was not noted till a single Fleet Air Arm aircraft flew in to look at the fjord and the Norwegian port of Bergen on the evening of 22 May. Admiral Tovey and his main force left Scapa Flow at once; this time it was the *Luftwaffe* who were prevented by the weather from observing the British movements and the ships' departures.

Despite rain and snow squalls, the *Bismarck* and her consort did not pass round Iceland and through the Denmark Strait unobserved. At 1922 hours on 22 May HMS *Suffolk* saw them steaming between her and the ice in the Strait, heading south-west towards the open Atlantic.

HMS *Suffolk*, under Captain Ellis, then began one of the most intense shadowing operations of all time. She was joined about an hour later by the cruiser that had been due to relieve her on patrol, HMS *Norfolk*, under Captain Phillips. Although briefly under fire from the German ship, the cruisers were able to send out a Sighting Report, and keep tracking, using smoke or the poor visibility to keep out of trouble. Meanwhile, HMS *Hood* and HMS *Prince of Wales* headed across from south of Iceland to intercept.

Then, everything began to go wrong. The shadowing cruisers lost the *Bismarck*, and Vice Admiral Holland in HMS *Hood* guessed wrongly about the direction in which to head for an encounter. When this encounter finally came about, he did not recognize it to be with the *Prinz Eugen*, which had taken the lead, whilst the *Bismarck* had dropped behind to deal with any shadowing cruiser that came too close.

The *Norfolk* and the *Suffolk* were actually a good fifteen miles behind when battle began. The role allotted them, which was to take out the *Prinz Eugen* while the two big British ships concentrated on the Bismarck, was thus way beyond their reach.

Worse errors were yet to come. When the British ships came under fire the much more vulnerable *Hood* was in the lead. What's more, neither the *Hood* nor the *Prince of Wales* were on a bearing that allowed them to use both their fore and aft sets of guns together. The *Hood* began firing at the *Prinz Eugen*, thinking it was the *Bismarck* because of its leading position – the German silhouettes were admittedly similar. Meanwhile the *Prince of Wales* engaged the *Bismarck* with her forward turrets only. From the start, both German ships concentrated their full sets of eight 15-inch guns and eight 8-inch guns on HMS *Hood*.

They immediately scored hits on HMS *Hood*, and started a fire. At 0600 hours, just as the two British ships altered course so as to bring all their turrets into action, the *Hood* blew up. Shells from the *Bismarck* had gone through her decks and hit a magazine. HMS *Hood* simply disintegrated. Only three men were rescued; Admiral Holland, Captain Kerr and all the other 1,419 officers and ratings were killed.

With hindsight it is clear that HMS *Prince of Wales* should have been in the lead. In the same way that three battlecruisers had been sunk at Jutland in World War I, so went the *Hood*, with shells crashing down on her decks. Speed was no substitute for armour.

Left: the *Bismarck* in all her glory. Not completed until August 1940, she displaced 42,000 tons and carried eight 15-inch guns, with a secondary armament of twelve 5.9-inch guns. She could steam at 30 knots, and had a range of well over 10,000 miles.

Top right: the British battlecruiser HMS *Hood*, pre-war flagship of the Royal Navy and, at the start of the War in 1939, one of the finest warships afloat. Built in 1920, she displaced 42,000 tons. Her armament was eight 15-inch guns, with a secondary armament of fourteen 4-inch guns. Despite her designation as a battle cruiser, she was really more of a fast battleship; though events would prove her to be too lightly armoured for that role. **Bottom right: HMS *Hood* engaged in pre-war manoeuvres with the British Home Fleet in the English Channel.** Most pre-war German battle-planning and naval exercises were held with the Hood as the enemy centrepiece that had to be defeated.

Top left: the *Bismarck* photographed at sea from her accompanying cruiser the *Prinz Eugen*. The latter was a heavy cruiser of some 15,000 tons with eight 8-inch guns, twelve 4-inch and 12 torpedo tubes.

Another photograph taken from the *Prinz Eugen* shows the *Bismarck* (bottom left) in action against HMS *Hood* and HMS *Prince of Wales*. The *Prinz Eugen* would soon leave her consort and head out into the Atlantic by herself.

Right: the British battleship HMS *King George V*, flagship of Admiral Tovey, commander in chief of the British Home Fleet. She led the hunt for the *Bismarck* and helped reduce her to a shattered hulk. Completed in 1940, the *King George V* carried ten 14-inch guns and sixteen 5.25-inch guns. Her heavily armoured decks and speed of 30 knots made her a fine fighting ship.

Both the *Bismarck* and the *Prince of Wales* had scored hits on each other. Neither knew the extent of the damage they had inflicted. Had the *Bismarck* known her only opponent had half her main guns out of action, she might have closed to finish her off. However, the *Prince of Wales* made smoke and turned away to await reinforcements.

As it happened these were heading for the scene at full speed. Admiral Tovey's force was some 300 miles to the southeast; Force 'H' from Gibraltar had left its convoy to head north, as had at least two other battleships and another aircraft carrier.

Bismarck had her 'shadows' with her again, and they reported she was heading south towards France or the Atlantic, rather than returning to go around Iceland and back to Germany. Aircraft launched from HMS *Victorious*, after being put off by coming unexpectedly across a neutral U.S. coastguard vessel in the area, did score one innefective torpedo hit on the *Bismarck*.

The *Prinz Eugen* was detached to continue on into the Atlantic alone. She did so, but a few days later developed engine trouble and had to sail to France. She need concern our story here no more.

Then the British lost the *Bismarck* again, mainly because they thought she was heading west into the Atlantic. She had actually turned for St. Nazaire, the only French port with repair yards big enough to handle a vessel of her size.

The net was tightening, but still the *Bismarck's* luck held. The British Admiralty made a mistake in its analysis of the direction from which the German battleship's signals were coming. It seemed she might be heading for the Iceland-Faeroes passage.

By the time it became clear that the *Bismarck* was heading for France, Admiral Tovey had already come to the same conclusion and set course accordingly. Bad weather prevented RAF Coastal Command from finding the German ship again till the morning of 26 May, 1942, – over three days since she was first sighted. Bismarck was less than 700 miles from Brest and the full protection of German aircraft and U-boats.

But Admiral Somerville's Force 'H' was closing. Although his World War I vintage battlecruiser HMS *Renown* had been ordered not to tangle with the *Bismarck,* there were still the planes from the *Ark Royal.*

Torpedoes might just reduce the *Bismarck's* speed, and allow Admiral Tovey and his two Home Fleet battleships to catch up. Sixteen aircraft from HMS *Ark Royal* took off in vile weather and, by mistake, launched their attack on the British cruiser HMS *Sheffield.* Luckily, drastic evasive action and a fault in the torpedoes' magnetic firing mechanism saved the *Sheffield.*

The torpedoes on the next flight of fifteen planes from the Ark Royal were equipped with contact charges. They were directed to their target by the *Sheffield.* In dreadful weather, high wind and poor visibility the aircraft attacked, despite heavy anti-aircraft fire.

It was a brave and magnificently uncoordinated attack. Thirteen torpedoes were dropped, two of which hit the *Bismarck.* One of them, like the torpedo hit scored from the *Illustrious* a day earlier, did little damage as it crashed into the ship's heavily-armoured side. However the other hit near the stern, wrecking the steering gear and jamming the rudder. The *Bismarck's* luck had at last run out. Admiral Lutjens signalled Germany: 'Can no longer manoeuvre. We fight to the last shell. Long live the Führer'.

British destroyers, led by Admiral Vian of Altmark fame, raced in and fired more torpedoes, further slowing the crippled battleship. Admiral Tovey now knew that the *Bismarck* could not escape. There was no need to risk a night action. At dawn next day his two battleships, HMS *Rodney* and HMS *King George V,* bore down on the *Bismarck* with their nine 16-inch guns and ten 14-inch guns.

The *Bismarck* fired her forward guns but soon these were hit, as were her control positions, both forward and aft. The *Bismarck* fought on, now using her aft guns singly. By 1000 hours even these were hit; the pride of the German Fleet was a burning wreck.

Two cruisers, HMS *Norfolk* and HMS *Dorsetshire,* closed, and fired torpedoes. It is not clear whether these, or scuttling charges placed by the German battleship's crew, did the trick, but shortly afterwards the *Bismarck's* bows rose up and she sank, stern first.

The *Bismarck* had put up a gallant fight, and went down with her colours still flying. With her went Admiral Lutjens, Captain Lindemann and all but 119 men out of the some 2,400 on board. In addition to Admiral Lutjen's staff, there were a number of prize crews on board.

New Yorkers read the news about the sinking of the Bismarck on a bulletin board in Times Square. The follow-up story suggesting that the *Prinz Eugen* would also be taken care of was not fulfilled at the time. The cruiser developed engine trouble, however, and could not continue her Atlantic raid, seeking safety in a French port.

Their job would have been to bring the *Bismarck's* captures home. There was also a posse of war correspondents there to describe her exploits to the world.

What lessons can be learned from this particular battle? First, that there is always going to be an element of luck involved. Luck as to where shells strike, as in the case of the *Hood*, or as to where a single torpedo hits, as in the case of the *Bismarck's* steering gear. Secondly, that the weather will always be a great influence, for good and for ill. It stopped aircraft from finding the *Bismarck* at first, but played a key role in the attacks later. Finally, despite two lapses, the 'shadowing' tactics employed by the cruisers were textbook examples of this procedure.

Perhaps the best aspect from the British point of view was the way in which the British Admiralty trusted the man on the spot, and did not override his decisions from headquarters. Admiral Tovey also let his flag officers take decisions – though he always greatly regretted not ordering HMS *Prince of Wales* to lead, and HMS *Hood* to follow.

There was courage too. From the slow-moving torpedo planes of HMS *Ark Royal* to the terrier-like attacks of Admiral Vian's destroyers, which could have been blown to smithereens even by the *Bismarck's* secondary armament. Nor must the courage of the men of the *Bismarck* herself be forgotten.

Though no-one knew it at the time, the loss of the *Bismarck* marked the end of German warship raids against convoys in the Atlantic. Her remaining warships would be used against the Russian convoys. British battleships were now free to travel to the Pacific.

RADAR AND SPECIAL WEAPONS

One of the hardest battles of the Second World War to describe, and certainly the hardest to illustrate, is the battle of the technologies. While some of the most modern, and the most ancient, of ships and aircraft battled against each other across the world, the boffins were working too. In their laboratories they competed to invent new equipment and new techniques with which to outwit the enemy.

For almost every invention a countermeasure was developed and in almost every case this was done within an incredibly short space of time. Generally these countermeasures also became known to the other side very quickly, and counter-countermeasures were instituted at once. Only occasionally did months elapse before one side or the other realised the enemy was using a new weapon, or was breaking their latest codes through intelligence work and cryptography.

Both the British and the Germans had developed rudimentary radar or R.D.F. (Radio Direction-Finding) before the War began. Radar would become a very powerful weapon both in the air and at sea, and today it is hard to envisage a time when radar was not an integral part of both navigation and warfare. Surprisingly, the Japanese were very slow to develop radar, and most of their ships operated without it during the Second World War.

The trouble with early radar was that it was large and bulky; suitable for use on an airfield or in a battleship, but too big for a destroyer or an aircraft. It also had a habit of going wrong or breaking down at crucial moments. What the Allies needed was a device that could detect a submarine on the surface at night or in poor visibility.

During the first winter of the War, two British scientists found a way to generate short electromagnetic waves, as opposed to the longer wavelengths used in ordinary radar. These could be measured in centimetres and, coupled with other improvements, led to what became known as centimetric radar.

This would be one of the more decisive inventions in the war against Donitz's U-boats. Ships, and more importantly aircraft, could now locate and attack submarines both at night and in thick fog and cloud. Even if they did not sink a U-boat every time, the attacks

often caused the U-boats to submerge just when they were recharging their batteries or giving their crews a breath of fresh air, as a change from the diesel-laden atmosphere in which they had to survive underwater.

Allied ship losses in early 1943 were staggering: some seventy ships sunk in February, over a hundred in March and another fifty in April. U-boat losses for these same months were a tolerable nineteen, fifteen and again fifteen respectively.

Suddenly things changed. U-boat sinkings of Allied ships in the Atlantic decreased dramatically between mid-May and September, while in May 1943 forty-one U-boats were sunk. Donitz withdrew his attack in that month, but still lost seventeen U-boats in June, thirty-seven in July and twenty-five in August.

Later the Germans would invent the 'snorkel', which allowed U-boats to stay submerged for much longer, and would improve the FAT acoustic torpedoes. These would turn around and come back seeking a ship if they failed to pick up the necessary propellor echoes on their first run. Despite these breakthroughs Admiral Donitz never succeeded in dominating the battle at sea in the way he had threatened to do in early 1943.

The advent of the acoustic torpedo had been anticipated, and the Allies countered with the 'foxer', a device that could be towed behind a ship and that made more noise than the ship's propellors. From then on, acoustic torpedoes destroyed many 'foxers', but far fewer ships.

Another device that came into operation during the War was the Leigh Light, a powerful searchlight carried by aircraft, which could surprise and illuminate a submarine on the surface. Yet another was the use by convoys of 'Snowflakes', star shells fired at the first sign of a U-boat attack to reveal the outline of any surfaced submarine.

It was, as aforementioned, a battle of device and counter-device. The Germans discovered the secret of centimetric radar when an Allied bomber equipped with it crashed in occupied territory. Within a short while the Germans had developed 'Metox', which a submarine could carry, and which picked up radar echoes coming from any searching aircraft. Another centimetric radar that could not be spotted by Metox was then developed, and thus the leapfrogging went on for five years.

At the very start of the War the Germans introduced their one secret weapon, the magnetic mine. They were unlike traditional sea mines, which had to be anchored to the bottom of the sea and only exploded on impact with a ship. Magnetic mines stayed on the bottom and then rose to the surface and exploded like a giant bomb when a ship passed over or near them. As they had no connecting chain, minesweepers could not use paravanes to cut this link and bring the mines to the surface where they could be destroyed by gunfire.

One of these magnetic mines was, however, washed ashore on the English coast in late November 1939, and was bravely taken apart by a naval bomb-disposal expert, Lieutenant J.G.D. Ouvry, RN. Its secrets were revealed and the inevitable countermeasure introduced. Degaussing was instituted, whereby an electric current was passed round a ship through cables, thereby demagnetising the vessel and making it immune to the mine. By March 1940, the peril of magnetic mines was almost over, though mines would again be used effectively several years later.

Just about every weapon used at sea was improved upon during the course of the Second World War. Surprisingly, no startling new weapons were introduced. It was almost always a case of developing existing ones, or of refining the techniques and tactics for their use. It is the smaller inventions of submarine and anti-submarine warfare that tend to capture the imagination, mainly because their effects, both in offence and defence, were so immediate.

Torpedoes underwent some remarkable changes as old versions proved fallible, and new versions were introduced to meet new tactical situations. The Germans, like the Americans later, had enormous problems with their early torpedoes, and had to rethink almost every principle they had been taught about their production and use.

One of Japan's greatest successes lay in her deadly 'Long Lance' torpedoes, twenty-four inches long and propelled by hydrogen. The more usual torpedoes were twenty-one inches long and were either propelled by compressed air or electrically-driven. Although other nations had experimented with Japanese-style hydrogen-propelled torpedoes, they were abandoned as too dangerous to operate. The Japanese took the risks, despite the casualties among operators, and enjoyed the torpedoes' success.

Depth charges, which still remained the main anti-submarine weapon, also underwent many transformations. Heavier types were manufactured, and others were designed to explode on impact rather than at a predetermined depth. New ways of launching them were introduced too. These included a throwing-machine, which could pitch them far ahead of a pursuing destroyer, and the 'Hedgehog' which could scatter a criss-cross pattern of twenty-four sixty-five-pound impact depth charges over a wide area. This latter, and its successor, the 'Squid', had the virtue of landing the depth charges ahead of a warship whose detection apparatus would otherwise have become ineffective as it overran its target. These new ways of dropping depth charges allowed the 'hunter-killer' escort groups to

The radar dome on a PT-boat housed the antenna of the radar set aboard the vessel. As much of the work of a PT-boat was done at night, the radar's electronic eye was invaluable for finding the way, indicating targets and warning of navigational dangers.

Left: work going on in the radar room aboard an American Essex-class aircraft carrier in the China Sea in December 1944. The Japanese, by contrast, were surprisingly slow to develop radar, and few of their ships carried even early versions of it. Had they chosen to apply their electronic skills to the development of radar, the Pacific War might have turned out quite differently.

The information coming from the radar room is being marked down on a vertical chart (right) in the radar plot room of an American aircraft carrier. Radar played a key part in helping the U.S.A. win the carrier battles of 1944 and 1945 in the Pacific.

devise new tactics for pursuing a submerged U-boat. Their efficiency soon showed up in the number of their kills.

The two anti-submarine devices which played key roles in the Battle of the Atlantic and elsewhere were 'Asdic' and 'Huff-Duff'.

'Asdic' was named after World War One's Allied Submarine Detection Investigation Committee. At the time, this had been trying unsuccessfully to come up with a way of locating submarines underwater. Eventually a method of transmitting supersonic pulses through the sea was developed. When the pulses encountered an underwater object, they were returned to the sender, making a characteristic, audible 'ping'. Using this apparatus, a ship's crew could work out the range and bearing of a submerged object.

'Asdic' did have disadvantages. It did not perform very well in rough weather, and its transmissions might equally well rebound from a whale, a dense shoal of fish, or even from certain water temperatures. Nor was it effective much beyond a mile, or if the destroyer using it was travelling at 20 knots or more. U-boat skippers learned to recognise both the 'ping' of 'Asdic' and its limitations, and to live with both.

More effective was High Frequency/ Direction Finding or HF/DF, commonly known as 'Huff-Duff'. This proved especially useful when U-boats were hunting in wolf-packs and either sending radio messages to each other or reporting back to their shore headquarters. Huff-Duff sets locked onto a submarine's transmitter and provided a bearing and a distance. Ideally two escorts would operate together to plot the intersecting point. With this device U-boats could be spotted at up to fifty miles, instead of the mile or so of an 'Asdic' contact, and their image displayed on a cathode-ray tube.

Perhaps the most important technological battles to affect sea warfare were in the realm of intelligence – the decryption and analysis of

High Frequency Direction Finder equipment, such as the set aboard the USS *Croatan* (left), played a vital part in the battle at sea, particularly against U-boats. A submarine using high frequency transmissions to communicate could be pinpointed by finding a bearing intersection between the signal heard at a coastal station and that aboard a ship, or between two ships each equipped with HF/DF, familiarly known as 'Huff-Duff'.

The combined kite-umbrella framework on top of a destroyer's mast (right) is the antenna of the High Frequency Direction Finder. HF/DF equipment aboard escort vessels played a key part in defeating Germany's U-boat campaign, particularly when U-boats were operating in 'wolf-packs' and had to signal to each other, or were being directed by signals from headquarters towards a convoy.

The U.S. Coast Guard cutter *Spencer* drops a depth charge (top left) whilst on convoy escort duty in the Atlantic in May 1943. Although depth charges had to land very close to a submarine to inflict serious damage, the explosion of one anywhere in the area had a singularly inhibiting effect on an underwater attacker.

Bottom left: the loading of a depth charge onto a launcher on the escort vessel HMS *Bittern*. Although the depth charge would be steadily developed throughout the War, it was still basically the same weapon used in World War I. Similarly, methods of launching depth charges would be considerably improved, but the principle remained unchanged.

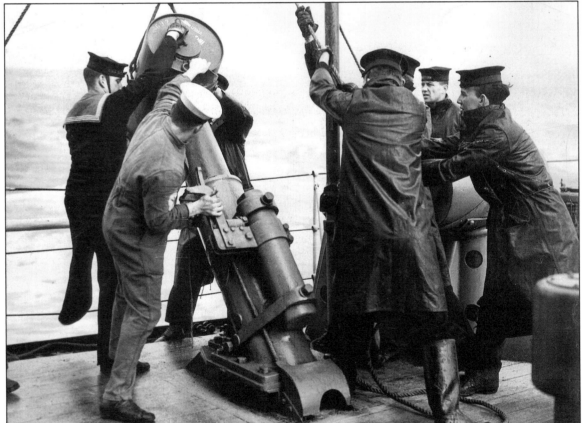

enemy radio messages and transmissions.

While the subject is too complicated to go into here, most people are now aware of the part that Britain's 'ULTRA' project played in the Second World War. This was the cover name given to information gained via the cryptographers who were reading Germany's secret 'Enigma' signals and disseminated at the very highest levels. This information was vital to Britain's war at sea and on land.

Reading Germany's signals had begun as early as mid-1940, but the techniques which speeded up the process became increasingly sophisticated as time went by. Then suddenly, in the summer of 1942, the Germans inserted a fourth wheel into their Enigma coding machines. The British cryptographers housed at Bletchley Park near Oxford were stymied. It took them several months to solve this new problem, and it was not till April 1943 that they were again penetrating Enigma.

What is not so generally well known is how successfully the Germans were reading the British naval code. They had been monitoring

British naval signals since the Abyssinian crisis in 1936, and were quite expert in British naval signalling procedure. By 1942 the Germans knew the projected sailing dates, route, destination, speed and size of escort of every British convoy. It was not till early 1943 that the British realised this, introduced a one-time pad, and effectively denied the Germans such knowledge for the rest of the War. Meanwhile each side had leapfrogged the other in intelligence successes.

In the Pacific, the Americans beat the Japanese hands down in terms of intelligence. U.S. cryptographers broke the Japanese navy code at a very early stage, and by 1942 could easily read a good sixty percent of all Japanese signals.

This penetration of communications was coupled with very effective use of direction-finding equipment. Any failure to maintain radio silence could be used to locate enemy dispositions. The Japanese tended to be very garrulous, and ship-to-ship and aircraft-to-ship chatting often gave away their positions quite

One weapon that was an entirely World War II innovation as an offensive weapon was the rocket. These were particularly useful for amphibious operations, such as the D-day landings and in Pacific island warfare, as they provided the equivalent of close artillery support for beach landings. Landing craft therefore carried rockets in great numbers (left).

Right: rockets being fired from an LSM (Landing Ship, Mechanised).

needlessly. The silent attack on Pearl Harbor was of course an exception.

Time and time again American intelligence learned of Japanese intentions in advance. Admiral Nimitz had been aware of Japanese plans to attack Port Moresby long before the battle of the Coral Sea. This advance warning allowed him to send reinforcements to the area in plenty of time.

In the Pacific, the United States would also benefit from British and other Allied inventions and developments, all of them already tried out under active service conditions. From August 1940, in fact, the Americans were privy to all their future ally's secrets in a sharing of intelligence and technical know-how that was historically unique. By contrast, the Germans hardly helped the Italians at all with radar, and only supplied the Japanese with help in this field when it was too late to make any difference.

Intelligence work, brilliant cryptography and a sharing of technologies played a key role in the Allies' sea battles.

PEARL HARBOR

Fifty years after the event it is easier to take an objective view as to what Japan's attack on Pearl Harbor meant to the Allies. Although 7 December, 1941, has gone down in history as a day of infamy and of treachery of the basest kind, it is now seen almost as a 'blessing in disguise' in terms of World War II.

War in the Pacific was inevitable in view of Japan's aggressive and expansionist policies in Southeast Asia. The manner and method of that war's beginning polarised public opinion in the U.S.A and in the rest of the Free World against the Axis powers.

Hitler and Mussolini, who were as surprised as anybody when the attack at Pearl Harbor took place, decided quite needlessly to declare war on the U.S.A. This left Congress, which had great doubts about fighting a two-ocean war, no choice but to accept that America must fight in Europe as well as in the Pacific.

In terms of the battle at sea, it marked the real moment of changeover from battles fought with guns to battles fought with aircraft. Against Pearl Harbor Japan launched the biggest force of carrier-borne aircraft ever to take part in a war at sea. Compared with the British attack on Taranto, which the Japanese had assiduously studied and in which twenty-one planes were used, Japan employed over 350 in her attack on America's great naval base in Hawaii.

The political manoeuvres that preceded 7 December are now all known. How, even as her envoys were negotiating peace in Washington, Japan's war fleet had sailed from the Kuriles. Led at sea by Vice Admiral Chuichi Nagumo, the fleet's centrepiece was two aircraft-carrier forces. These totalled six of the largest and fastest vessels of their kind – the *Akagi*, the *Kaga*, the *Hiryu*, the *Soryu*, the *Shokaku* and the *Zuikaku*. Between them, they housed some 430 bombers, torpedo-bombers and fighters. Their crews were fully-trained professionals, many of them already having had combat experience in China. The carriers were protected by two battleships, the *Hiyei* and the *Kirishima*, two heavy cruisers and a destroyer flotilla of ten ships.

The aircrews trained for this operation for months, and knew the model of Pearl Harbor and its defences intimately. It is said that so

fierce and realistic was their training that they actually lost more aircraft during the rehearsals than they did on the day.

Anchored in Pearl Harbor was the great bulk of the American Pacific Fleet: eight out of nine battleships, and over eighty other vessels. The battleships were mainly tied up in pairs along the quayside. It was a Sunday in peacetime. Most of the crews were ashore, and most people were asleep, when the attack began.

There will probably always be some controversy about how much the highest echelons in Washington knew of Japanese intentions. They knew an attack was likely but probably not where or when.

In the north of the island of Oahu (Pearl Harbor is on its southern coast) a couple of army men finishing their night shift at a radar

Almost exactly a year before the Japanese attack on Pearl Harbor, a series of publicity pictures were issued by the military authorities to present the base as the U.S.A.'s Hawaiian stronghold. The sentry in the still (left) was described as typical of the thousands of men guarding what was described as America's Gibraltar. The series also included a picture of the searchlights of the U.S. battlefleet lighting up the peacetime night sky over Pearl Harbor (top right); a picture that the events of 7 December, 1941, would render unfortunate.

While the Americans were enjoying their last few months of peace, the Japanese were planning their attack on Pearl Harbor. The Japanese air crews used a model mock-up (bottom far right) to familiarize themselves with 'Battleship Row' at Ford Island. It is said that the Japanese rehearsals for the attack were so fierce and realistic that they lost more aircraft in practices than the twenty-nine they lost on the day itself.

Bottom right: a Japanese view of the attack on Pearl Harbor on 7 December, 1941, taken from one of the aircraft actually involved in it.

station detected a large 'blip' on their screens. They were not particularly alarmed, thinking it was probably a naval exercise they had not been told about; inter-service rivalry had a habit of complicating communications in Hawaii. When they eventually found an officer to report to he was similarly unconcerned, as he was expecting a flight of B-17s to arrive that day.

The first strike wave of 184 Japanese aircraft went into the attack a few minutes before 8.00 a.m. local time, 7 December, 1941. Drilled on exactly which targets to attack, they swung across the harbour and launched their bombs and torpedoes. They did so unopposed, for it was not till the bombing was well under way that there was any response from the watch on duty in the ships below.

None of the battleships escaped unscathed, though the USS *Maryland* and USS *Pennsylvania* were damaged to a lesser extent. The USS *Arizona* was hit first, and badly; her forward magazine exploded and she split in two. Forty-seven officers and 1,056 men died, including her captain and Rear Admiral Isaac C. Kidd.

The ancient World War I USS *Oklahoma* was the next most serious victim. She was hit by five torpedoes and capsized, taking twenty officers and 395 men with her. Several bombs and a torpedo hit the USS *Nevada* while the USS *West Virginia* was also torpedoed. The USS *California* and the USS *Tennessee* were also damaged. Three cruisers and three destroyers were disabled, and the former battleship *Utah*, downgraded to a target ship, was also hit.

One hour after the first attack, a second strike wave of 170 Japanese aircraft arrived over Pearl Harbor. They continued attacking the warships and also the airfields, which proved to be in a similar state of unreadiness. Most of the aircraft were undispersed, lined up wing tip to wing tip, and forming sitting targets. Nearly

Left: a view of burning buildings and ships after the surprise attack on Pearl Harbor by 350 carrier-borne Japanese aircraft.

Right: an often reproduced but nonetheless most spectacular photograph taken during the bombing of Pearl Harbor.

Bottom left: the smoking hulk of the battleship USS *Arizona*, which was the first ship to be badly hit and which was split in two by an explosion. Forty-seven officers and 1,056 men died on board, including her captain and Rear Admiral Isaac C. Kidd.

Top left: two further battleships that were bombed at Pearl Harbor – the USS *West Virginia* and the USS *69 Tennessee*. Though disabled to varying degrees by the attack, they were amongst those ships worth repairing and were eventually sent back into action.

Right: blasted by bombs and torpedoes, the battleship USS *California* settles slowly into the mud. Of the eight battleships hit, two, the *Arizona* and the *Oklahoma*, would never sail again, but the others would all return to service eventually.

200 U.S. aircraft were destroyed or damaged on the ground.

It was a brilliantly planned and executed attack and represented a victory for the aircraft carrier over the battleship. The Japanese lost twenty-nine aircraft, fifty-five crew members, and five midget submarines. Admiral Yamamoto, whose overall plan it was, had knocked out his enemy's capital ships in one fell swoop.

However his men had not hit any American aircraft carriers. By a lucky chance, the USS *Enterprise* and USS *Lexington*, which would otherwise have been with the battleships, were engaged in delivering aircraft to Midway and Wake. The third aircraft carrier, the USS *Saratoga*, and the ninth and last battleship of the Pacific Fleet, the USS *Colorado*, were on the west coast of the U.S.A.

Another misfortune for the Japanese was that their plans had neglected to include the destruction of the oil terminals and storage-tanks. Had these gone up too, the American Fleet would have been even more severely handicapped. As things stood, the American Navy had lost two battleships forever: the *Arizona* would be left at the bottom of the harbour, and the *Oklahoma* would prove not

61

to be worth repairing. The other six, though disabled to varying degrees, would all return to service. There were twenty cruisers and sixty-five destroyers still battleworthy.

The Japanese Fleet turned away, leaving the Americans to bury their dead and succour their wounded, many of whom had ghastly burns from flaming fuel. 2,400 had died: 1,763 men on the ships and another 700 people or more on shore.

With hindsight we can say that the aforementioned 'blessing in disguise' took several forms. Because the battle occurred in a harbour, most of the ships could be reclaimed. Had the same devastation taken place on the high seas, the battleships would have gone to the bottom, taking far more of their crews with them. The aircraft carriers were spared to fight another day, as were nearly all the cruisers and destroyers, together with their crews. Lessons were learned, and 'avenge Pearl Harbor' became a rallying cry and a cause for a whole nation.

Although the Japanese put their major effort into attacking Pearl Harbor, they simultaneously attacked other American and Allied targets. Guam, which was surrounded by Japanese islands, surrendered within three days; Wake fought back but was captured on 23 December.

In fact, the Japanese, most of whose forces were still fighting in China, launched five separate new campaigns: Hong Kong; the Philippines; Burma; Malaya and Singapore; and the Dutch East Indies. Hong Kong held out only until Christmas.

If further proof of battleship vulnerability were needed, it came only a few days later, when Japanese land-based aircraft sank both the British battleship HMS *Prince of Wales* and the battlecruiser HMS *Renown* off Malaya.

Admiral Tom Phillips had taken his two capital ships up from Singapore to try and interrupt a Japanese landing. At 11.00 a.m. on 10 December, 1941, some 250 miles north of Singapore, and with no air cover, the two capital ships were attacked. Nearly one hundred Japanese aircraft were employed from airfields near Saigon, in Vietnam. It was over almost as quickly as Pearl Harbor. Both ships went down, taking 840 of those onboard with them, including Admiral Phillips.

On both land and sea the Japanese could hardly be checked anywhere. General MacArthur in the Philippines probably delayed them most, retreating by way of the fortress peninsula of Bataan. The capture of Malaya and Singapore, which Japan expected to take one hundred days, was over in considerably less. Singapore fell on 15 February, 1942, with the capture of 130,000 British and Commonwealth prisoners.

Japanese ships later swept into the Indian Ocean, as far as Ceylon, which was now the British naval headquarters. They did not, however, find the British Far East Fleet, which had left harbour to face the enemy on the open seas. After attacks on bases at both ends of Ceylon, the Japanese withdrew to Singapore. Meanwhile their army colleagues were finding rich pickings in the Dutch East Indies and in the island archipelagos beyond.

Although battleships were the main targets, other ships were sunk or damaged, amongst them the destroyers USS *Downes* and USS *Cassin* (left). The battleship USS *Pennsylvania*, which was only lightly damaged, can be seen in the background.

Nearly 200 U.S. aircraft were destroyed or damaged in the Japanese attack on the airfields around Pearl Harbor (right). Hangars suffered badly too. Most of the aircraft were stacked wing tip to wing tip, and the American air forces were as unprepared as the fleet for the attack.

In addition to twenty-nine aircraft, the Japanese lost five two-man midget submarines, such as the one washed up on the beach at Pearl Harbor (left). Although the submarines achieved almost nothing, all their crews were highly decorated and praised, which would prove a source of grievance to some of the air crews, who felt their own highly successful contribution was comparatively less well rewarded.

BATTLE OF THE JAVA SEA

The Battle of the Java Sea on 26/27 February, 1941, was a disaster. If nothing else, it proved that heroism and seamanship are not always enough, and that victory generally goes to those who can produce the largest concentration of big guns, torpedoes and aircraft. This time, air power was not a major factor, though, as was usual at this stage of the War, the Allies were operating with virtually no direct air support.

It was a very mixed Allied force too, with ships ranging from useful 8-inch gun cruisers to destroyers that dated back to World War I. In its very multinationality lay additional reasons for the defeat.

Led by Dutch Rear Admiral Karel Doorman, this ABDA (Australian British Dutch American) force consisted of two heavy cruisers, HMS *Exeter* and USS *Houston*, three light cruisers with 6-inch guns, the Australian HMAS *Perth* and the Dutch cruisers, the *De Ruyter*, which was Doorman's flagship, and the *Java*.

Additionally there were nine destroyers: four American, three British and two Dutch. The problems arose because the fleet had never worked together before, but had merely been assembled from the very few ships available in

the area. Each nationality relied on very different communication practices and procedures. Inevitably they all had trouble understanding each other's signals throughout the action.

The Japanese plans to create an empire in Southeast Asia are aptly described by Richard Hough in his book, *The Longest Battle*, as 'outrageous in scale, brilliant in conception, and so far successful in execution'. These plans included seizing the wealth of the Dutch East Indies by moving southwards from Singapore, by land through Sumatra and by sea to Java. The eventual target was Australia.

By mid-February 1941 Sumatra was theirs, and they were poised to invade the next large island in the chain, Java. Here some 30,000 Dutch and other troops faced the Japanese 16th Army. In a last desperate attempt to meet this threat, Rear Admiral Doorman's fleet headed out of its base at Sourabaya to try and stop any landings.

There was only one possible outcome. Before the ABDA force had much of a chance of reaching the transports, they were engaged by a more powerful Japanese force. This outnumbered the Allies about two to one in 8-

The British heavy cruiser HMS *Exeter* (top left), which had distinguished herself at the Battle of the River Plate over a year before, was one of the casualties of the Battle of the Java Sea. Outnumbered two to one, the *Exeter* and the USS *Houston* took the brunt of the Japanese attack, and the *Exeter* had to pull out of the battle and try to reach Australia for repairs. She would be sunk on 1 March, 1941, as she tried to make her way southwards.

Right: the *Exeter*'s crew in happier days, being addressed by Winston Churchill, then First Lord of the Admiralty.

Although she survived the actual Battle of the Java Sea, the USS *Houston* (bottom left) would be sunk a day later after sinking two Japanese transports. An Augusta-class cruiser of 9,200 tons she carried nine 8-inch guns and twelve 5-inch guns.

inch guns, a superiority the Japanese would exploit.

Standing off and shooting from a range of about thirteen miles, they concentrated their fire on HMS *Exeter* and USS *Houston* – the only two ships that could respond at that range. The *Exeter* was hit in the engine room, and had to pull out. The victor of the Battle of the River Plate would be sunk a couple of days later, on 1 March. She went down together with her escort, the U.S. destroyer *Pope*, as she tried to make her way to Australia through the Sunda Strait.

The British destroyer *Electra* was another early casualty. Set ablaze by big shells, she was finished off, still fighting gallantly, by the more modern, more powerful Japanese destroyers. The Dutch destroyer *Kortenaer* was torpedoed and sunk, and her consort damaged when one of her own depth charges exploded under

her stern. The British destroyer HMS *Jupiter* was lost when she ran into a Dutch minefield.

By this stage, the Japanese had closed and both Dutch cruisers had been sunk, Rear Admiral Doorman going down with the *De Ruyter.* Of the cruisers, only the USS *Houston* and HMAS *Perth* still survived, and they made their way to the island's capital of Batavia, now Jakarta.

A few days later they managed to sink two Japanese transports and two other ships, but as they moved through the Sunda Strait towards Australia they too were attacked, and sunk.

On 5 March, Batavia had been declared an 'open city'. A few days later all Java surrendered. A gallant and sacrificial effort by the small Allied force had probably not even delayed the irrepressible Japanese.

Two other lessons were learned at the Battle of the Java Sea. The first was the way in which the Japanese compensated for their lack of radar by using seaplanes for reconnaissance. While the Allies were failing to communicate even with one another, Japanese seaplanes were out and about everywhere reporting back to their big-gun cruisers the whereabouts of all their opponents.

The second was the noteworthy success of the Japanese in the deadly use of their 'Long Lance' 24-inch torpedoes. These were oxygen powered, effective within a range of up to 22,000 yards and travelled at speeds of well over 40 knots.

As mentioned before, other navies had experimented with these oxygen-powered torpedoes, but most had rejected their use as too dangerous. The Japanese had persevered, accepting a rate of casualties in their handling that probably no other navy would tolerate, and this paid off in the Java Sea.

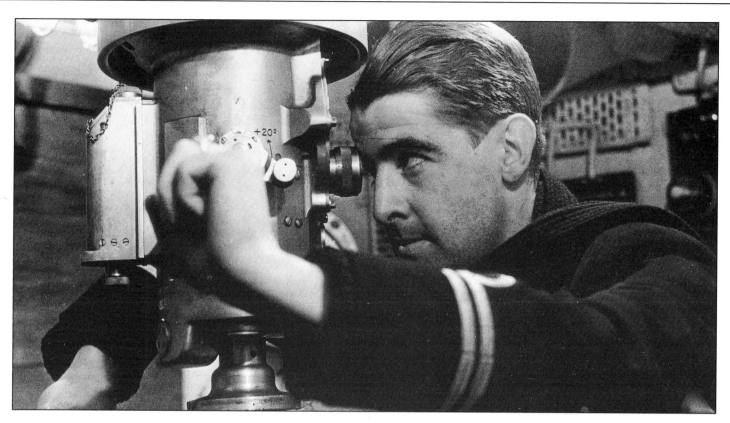

BATTLE OF THE CORAL SEA

The Battle of the Coral Sea in May 1942 was the first battle ever fought at sea between two fleets that never even saw each other.

The closest they ever came to meeting was about fifty miles. The deciding weapons were no longer shells from big guns, but bombs and torpedoes from planes operating from aircraft carriers.

The Coral Sea lies off the northeast coast of Australia. It is encircled by a string of islands that separate it from the rest of the Pacific: Papua New Guinea; the Bismarck Archipelago and New Britain; and the Solomons and the New Hebrides.

By April 1942, the Japanese controlled the islands of the Bismarck Archipelago and were moving into the Solomons – Bougainville, Tulagi, and Guadalcanal. Their main base was Rabaul in New Britain, and they held the north of Papua New Guinea. Their next target on that huge island territory was Port Moresby in the south, to be followed by Australia. Several Japanese naval forces were in the area, covering the landings at Tulagi and escorting the troopships heading for Port Moresby. Others were getting into position to head off any Allied forces that might interfere with their sea-borne invasions.

Together they amounted to two large aircraft carriers, the 30,000-ton sister ships *Shokaku* and *Zuikaku* of some, one smaller 15,000-ton carrier, the *Shoho*, nine cruisers and fifteen destroyers.

The overall Japanese commander, Vice Admiral Inouye, thought the most he would face would be one aircraft carrier, plus cruisers.

However, the American commander in chief in the Pacific, Admiral Nimitz, knew of the Japanese plans through the breaking of their naval code. Nimitz therefore despatched

The Battle of the Coral Sea was the first naval battle in which the opposing forces never came within fifty miles of each other. It was a carrier battle fought between forces of almost equal size, and if tactically it was a 'tie', strategically it was an American victory. Left: SBD Dauntless aircraft safely back on the USS *Lexington* after a strike against the Japanese carriers.

Top right: although the carrier was damaged by Japanese attackers, most of USS *Lexington*'s aircraft were already back on board. After the Japanese attack, destroyers (bottom right) removed those crewmen not needed for fire fighting from the USS *Lexington*. Destroyers also pumped water onto the starboard side of the carrier to try and stem the fires.

another carrier, the USS *Lexington*, plus two more 8-inch gun cruisers and five destroyers from Pearl Harbor as reinforcements. The aircraft carrier USS *Yorktown* was already in the Coral Sea, escorting cruisers and destroyers.

In the following four days of manoeuvering and fighting, the opposing forces were very roughly equal. The Japanese had one small carrier extra, and a slight edge in the number of cruisers and destroyers. However, they also had Japanese transports to protect.

The Japanese began by occupying Tulagi, without meeting any opposition. In fact, the senior American commander there, Rear Admiral Fletcher, on the *Yorktown*, did not learn of this until the evening after the landing. Even then he learned it only from a land-based reconnaisance aircraft.

At this stage of the War, U.S. carrier-borne aircraft could not operate at night; their pilots were not trained for night flying. Next day, however, nearly a hundred U.S. carrier-borne aircraft raided Tulagi, sinking a Japanese destroyer and three other smaller vessels in the harbour. First blood to the Americans.

This success was partly due to the Japanese admiral's decision to use his aircraft carriers to ferry a small number of fighter aircraft to Rabaul instead of moving at speed into the Coral Sea.

The next two days saw the two aircraft-carrier fleets searching the Coral Sea for each other. At one stage they were as close as fifty miles, but never within gun range. Identifying ships from the air is seldom easy, and visibility over these two days was not good. Both sides would make a number of mistakes of identification or communication. Had these errors not been evenly balanced, the battle might have been settled at an early stage.

Japanese search planes were the first to find an enemy ship at sea, a tanker from which the USS *Yorktown* had just refuelled, together with its escorting destroyer. However, these were described to Admiral Inouye as an aircraft carrier and a cruiser. Thus they became the target for a full-scale Japanese attack, which sank them both.

Not to be outdone, an American reconnaisance plane from the *Yorktown* found what it thought to be two cruisers and two destroyers. They were reported, this time as a result of a coding error, as two aircraft carriers and four cruisers. The Americans therefore launched a full attack, using just under one hundred bombers and torpedo-carrying planes.

In fact, the force that they had found was one commanded by Rear Admiral Goto, coming down to support the Japanese transports heading for Port Moresby. It included just one small aircraft carrier, the *Shoho*, under Captain Izawa, which was hit within minutes by a dozen bombs and seven torpedoes, and sank. About a hundred of her crew were rescued by an accompanying Japanese destroyer.

The sinking of the *Shoho*, which left each side with two large carriers, would be more important than was at first thought. It led to the recall of the Japanese force bound for Port Moresby.

Meanwhile, a force of cruisers, two Australian and one American, had been sent to intercept these transports and their escorting force. As these had turned back, they could not of course be found. Instead the cruisers came under heavy attack from both land-based Japanese aircraft and, by mistake, from U.S. Army Air Force planes flying out of Australia. Excellent ship handling enabled them to escape the attentions of both enemies and 'friends', though the Japanese claimed one battleship sunk and another torpedoed.

One must be careful not to overemphasise the muddle in battles of this kind, but to remind oneself that brave men were hazarding, and often losing, their lives in order to try and find and defeat the enemy. The next attack had to contend with that ever-present and impartial enemy – bad weather.

The Japanese aircraft carriers sent out a strike force to find the Americans. When they had not done so by dusk, they were forced to jettison their bombs and torpedoes and return home. On their way back they were intercepted by American fighters which shot nine down. Another six that tried to land on the *Yorktown*, believing her to be Japanese, were also destroyed. A further eleven Japanese aircraft were lost attempting night landings once they had found their own carriers. Only seven aircraft survived. It was not until 8 May, 1942, that the final battle was fought. By then each side had about 120 planes left. Each side's carriers had a roughly similar force of cruisers around them in defence.

For once the weather was less than impartial. The Japanese carriers were hidden by low rain clouds; the American carriers were exposed in

The beginning of the end for the USS *Lexington* in the Battle of the Coral Sea in May 1942. All her crew have now abandoned ship, and fires rage both above and below decks and in her superstructure. Hours later, the U.S. destroyer *Phelps* was ordered to sink the stricken carrier, and did so with five torpedoes.

bright sunshine. Both sides launched attacks.

The Americans failed to find the aircraft carrier *Zuikaku* but scored three bomb hits on the *Shokaku*. They lost thirty-three planes. The Japanese were more successful. They scored one bomb hit on the *Yorktown*, and hit the *Lexington* with two bombs and two torpedoes. They too lost some thirty planes to American fighters and anti-aircraft fire.

The attempt to save the damaged USS *Lexington* is part of history, and has been well documented in photographs. A stricken aircraft carrier is a particularly sad sight. Her bulky, flat-topped, apparently top-heavy shape gives her an extra air of vulnerability.

The *Lexington*, under Captain Sherman, though her engines were still intact, was listing to port, and was on fire in several places. Sherman was convinced there was a chance of saving her, although leaking petrol later caused one explosion, and others followed. Finally she began to lose power and further fire fighting became impossible.

Some four and a half hours after the first major explosion, the order was given to abandon ship. Destroyers rescued most of her crew, though 216 had been killed either in the Japanese attack or during the earlier struggle to save her.

Who then won the Battle of the Coral Sea ?

The Japanese sank the 35,000-ton American aircraft carrier *Lexington*; the Americans the 15,000-ton *Shoho*. Both sides had a large carrier damaged: the *Yorktown* was repaired within a month; the Japanese *Shokaku* remained in dock for over two months.

More importantly the Japanese were to find themselves ill prepared for the next big aircraft-carrier battle which was to come a month later at Midway. The damage to the *Shokaku*, and the loss of planes and trained crews on both her and the *Zuikaku*, meant neither of these two Coral Sea aircraft carriers was battleworthy.

If these considerations made the Battle of the Coral Sea a tie in a tactical sense, strategically it was an American victory. The Japanese were forced to call off their plans to sail round Papua New Guinea and capture Port Moresby – their chosen base for an attack on Australia.

The battle also constituted the first real check to the great Japanese drive south through the Pacific. At every point until then, from that first surprise attack on Pearl Harbor onwards, it had been a ruthlessly successful campaign.

BATTLE OF MIDWAY

Midway has been described as the first and biggest full-scale aircraft-carrier battle of all time. It was not. The Battle of the Coral Sea exactly a month earlier was the first, and bigger battles would follow. In the Battle of the Philippine Sea in June 1944, nine Japanese carriers faced twelve of those from the U.S.

Midway was important, constituting a decisive turning point in checking Japan's advance across the Pacific. It was indubitably an American victory, but it could easily have gone either way.

The exact strategies and detailed studies of the aircraft strikes have been exhaustively covered in such books as *Miracle at Midway* by Gordon W. Prange (McGraw Hill, 1982) and the fourth volume of *History of United States Naval Operations in World War II* by Samuel Eliot Morison.

These accounts make interesting and sobering reading, as one realises just how many brave and gallant pilots and crews went to their deaths in this battle. Many of the American planes that were thrown into the fight, especially the TBF (Avenger) aircraft, which were making their debut, suffered heavy losses. They stood little chance against the powerful, highly-manoeuverable Japanese Zero fighters. The TBD (Devastator) torpedo bombers suffered equally badly. Midway proved to be a battle in which the shortcomings of many American aircraft were revealed. Only the Dauntless dive bombers proved truly effective, and they are credited with settling the outcome of the carrier battle.

It was the Japanese who chose Midway to be the battleground. The Japanese plan, carefully worked out by Admiral Yamamoto, was to capture the island, and lure the American fleet out into the Pacific before destroying it. The Japanese had missed finding the American aircraft carriers at Pearl Harbor,

so this would be their chance to stage a confrontation on a chosen site and sink them.

The Japanese sent out a huge fleet of more than eighty surface warships, plus another force that would make a diversionary attack on the Aleutian Islands off Alaska. Admiral Yamamoto was flying his flag aboard the biggest battleship in the world, the 64,000-ton *Yamato*. His main force included two other battleships, a light carrier, two seaplane carriers – each with a dozen midget submarines aboard – a light cruiser and eight protecting destroyers.

A guard force of four more battleships, two cruisers and a dozen destroyers was sailing independently. This was for use either with the main force or to be detached to protect the Aleutian expedition if needed.

However, the centrepiece was the first carrier striking force, commanded by Vice Admiral Chiuchi Nagumo, the victor at Pearl Harbor. This comprised four aircraft carriers organised in two divisions: the *Akagi* and the *Kaga*, the *Hiryu* and the *Soryu*. Between them they were carrying some 260 aircraft, divided almost equally between dive bombers, torpedo bombers and Zero fighters. The carrier fleet had a supporting force of two more battleships, both heavy and light cruisers, and another dozen destroyers.

Finally, there was the Midway invasion force itself, comprising two more battleships, nine heavy and light cruisers, an escort carrier, numerous destroyers and a fleet of transports carrying troops. There were other supporting forces including oilers and supply ships, seaplane carriers, and minesweepers.

Last but not least there were a submarine tender and ten submarines. These would spread out in a great fan-shaped forward patrol east of Midway, ready to report any American ships coming on the scene.

To oppose this formidable array, the Americans had some twenty-eight ships. They were centred on two carrier task forces, TF16 with USS *Enterprise* and USS *Hornet*, and TF17 with USS *Yorktown*. The three U.S. carriers had 233 aircraft between them, plus support from a goodly number of land-based aircraft on Midway, including B-19s (Flying Fortresses) and B-26s. The rest of the American warships were a mixture of cruisers and destroyers, together with nineteen submarines.

The Americans were heavily outnumbered and would have to be very careful not to be lured into the trap the Japanese had set for them. They had, however, some unseen advantages. U.S. intelligence was way ahead of the Japanese in providing information about

The USS *Yorktown* under attack during an early stage of the Battle of Midway on 4/6 June, 1942. One of the Japanese errors was to try and combine two objectives at the same time: the capture of the island of Midway and the destruction of the American aircraft carrier fleet in the Pacific.

During the battle, the USS Yorktown, flagship of Rear-Admiral Frank J. Fletcher, was hit and set on fire by Japanese carrier-borne aircraft.

enemy dispositions. In addition, the American carriers were equipped with radar, which gave them that extra advance warning that could make the difference between success and failure in a carrier fight.

As it turned out, the Japanese made a great number of mistakes, mainly attributable to the arrogance arising from their long series of triumphs in the Pacific and Indian Oceans.

The Americans would prove to have two further advantages: luck, and an admiral who outthought and outfought his Japanese opposite number. In fact, there were two American admirals who hardly put a foot wrong in this engagement: Rear Admiral Frank J. Fletcher aboard the *Yorktown* and Rear Admiral Raymond A. Spruance aboard the *Enterprise*. Spruance is generally given most of the credit, but Rear Admiral Fletcher, who was the senior of the two, gave Spruance just the right amount of support and freedom in his decision making. This of course is not always the case when two commanders of equal rank operate in tandem.

For the naval historian, the interest in Midway inevitably lies in what might have happened if things had worked out differently. Hindsight also provides us with an opportunity to judge what should have been done, and also to wonder why things that seem so obvious to us

now were not taken into consideration on 4 June, 1942, and on the two days which followed.

It seems clear to us now that Admiral Yamamoto's decision to bring up the rear with his main force was a mistake. At the time when it might have played a part in searching out the American carriers, it was miles away and, after the carrier battle had gone against the Japanese, the force was handled very indecisively.

For all the part the main force and the smaller carriers dispersed throughout the various Japanese groups played in the Battle of Midway, they might just as well have stayed at home and saved the fuel. Everything was left to Nagumo's First Air Fleet.

The first bit of American luck, or bad Japanese management, was the two American carrier task forces getting into position undetected, well to the northwest of Midway. The Japanese submarines were almost two days late in taking up their patrol arc east of Midway. The second Japanese failing was in not using reconnaissance aircraft to their full capacity.

Lacking radar, the Japanese were completely reliant on reconnaissance work, yet it came low in their priorities. Little training was given to pilots in this role, which was

looked down on as a defensive measure not in keeping with the offensive attitude of the Imperial Japanese Navy. A ten percent limit had been placed on the number of aircraft used for reconnaissance.

Thereafter, whilst Vice Admiral Nagumo made several tactical errors, Rear Admiral Spruance seemed to make the right decision every time. When American aircraft spotted Japanese forces heading for Midway, Spruance correctly judged that they were transports or escort forces, not the key aircraft-carrier group that he was to stop reaching Midway.

The Japanese, still not suspecting that American carriers were anywhere near at hand, then launched their first attack on Midway. 108 carrier-borne aircraft comprimising a mixture of level bombers, dive bombers and a strong fighter escort, took off.

Midway was ready for them. Its own bombers took off and its fighters and anti-aircraft guns put up a good defence, despite the superiority of the Zero fighters. Not as much damage was

done to the three airfields there as had been feared, and at least nine Japanese planes were shot down and another two dozen damaged.

The returning force signalled: 'There is need for a second attack wave'. Nagumo had kept half his strike aircraft loaded with torpedoes to deal with the American aircraft carrier, or carriers, should these appear. He then decided to unload the torpedoes and load his aircraft up with bombs instead.

This illustrates the problems arising from giving a naval force two separate tasks to carry out. Nagumo was told that his priority was to smash Midway so that it could be captured, but also that he should lure the American carrier force into the open and destroy it.

While he pondered his priorities, his ships were being attacked by land-based aircraft from Midway, albeit a very motley force of six TBF (Avengers), four B-26 bombers, and Vindicators and B-17s. Although several near misses occurred and some optimistic claims for hits made, the attackers succeeded only in

Japanese problems did not end with the carrier battle, in which all four carriers of Vice Admiral Nagumo's First Carrier Striking Force were eliminated. The following day, two of the heavy Mogami-class cruisers that had been part of the Midway bombardment force collided and were badly damaged. On 6 June, the two cruisers were found by U.S. aircraft and bombed (top and bottom left). The Mikuma sank, and the 69 Mogami, though seriously hit, was recovered and would be converted to an aircraft-carrying cruiser. She was finally sunk by U.S. aircraft, off the Philippines in October 1944.

irritating the Japanese. The Americans suffered heavy losses. The failure of these bombing attacks and of the fighters defending Midway added to Japanese overconfidence. Perhaps in this, and in the distraction they provided, lay the attacks' major contribution to victory.

Space allows only a brief summing-up of the actual battle here. Suffice to say, Spruance got it right again. He took his chief of staff's advice to strike at Nagumo just as the latter's planes returned from Midway, and to go for them with his full strength. 116 planes took off from the Hornet and the Enterprise. The Yorktown's would follow an hour later.

It worked. Nagumo now knew that there were American aircraft carriers in the offing, and that he would have to attack them next, and not Midway. Before Nagumo had decided whether to send off his strike force, only half of whom were armed with torpedoes, or to delay, take on his returning aircraft and rearm the rest, the Americans were on their way.

American bravery, and luck, settled the carrier battle, and thus the Battle of Midway. The bravery came in the attacks pressed home by the torpedo-carrying planes once they found the carriers, which not all did. The luck came in an unorthodox search manoeuvre executed by the dive-bombers, which found the Japanese where they were not expected to be. Luck played its part again when the Yorktown's dive bombers arrived to attack at the same moment, a piece of unplanned 'co-ordination'.

Victory was mainly due to the dive bombers' attacks. The Kaga was hit first just as planes were taking off, then two more bombs crashed through into the hangars below, fires were started and power lost. All those on her bridge were killed. A fourth bomb sealed her fate. Nagumo's flagship, the Akagi was also hit several times, and great damage inflicted when stacks of bombs not cleared away from the rearming exploded. The Akagi, by then a hulk, was sunk next morning by Japanese destroyers.

The Yorktown's dive bombers also accounted for the Soryu. She was reduced to a wreck, abandoned by her crew, and despatched that evening by the U.S. submarine Nautilus. Having had three of his four aircraft carriers put out of action within six minutes, Admiral Nagumo might understandably have withdrawn at this stage, but he did not. Instead

he ordered two strikes against the American carriers from the surviving Hiryu.

Most of the forty attacking aircraft were shot down either by American fighters or by anti-aircraft fire, but a few got through. The Yorktown was hit by three bombs and two torpedoes and had to be abandoned. However, aircraft from the Enterprise found the Hiryu and inflicted so much damage that she barely survived the night, and actually sank the following day.

Admiral Yamamoto seemed determined to continue to make a fight of it. He called down his small carriers from the Aleutians, and brought up his heavy cruisers to join the main fleet. However he then appears to have lost heart. His aircraft-carrier force had after all suffered disastrous losses: four ships, 250 planes and over 2,000 officers and men. He cancelled a planned bombardment of Midway, and signalled his fleet to withdraw to Japan.

The Japanese troubles were not over. Two cruisers from the Midway bombardment force of Vice Admiral Takeo Kurita's close support group, the Mikuma and the Mogami, collided when turning to avoid an attack from the U.S. submarine Tambor. Both were badly damaged. They were found at 0800 next morning, 6 June, 1942, by Spruance's dive-bombers. The Mikuma was sunk, but the Mogami managed to get back to Truk.

Admiral Yamamoto now changed his mind again, and ordered cruisers to go after the U.S. carriers, turning his battle fleet back to provide support. Spruance again showed exemplary judgement. He withdrew to the east, to refuel from his fleet train and to avoid being trapped into a fight with surface ships. He had done his job.

The USS Yorktown, which some commentators claimed had been prematurely abandoned, was being towed by a minesweeper, and a salvage crew were working to save her. The U.S. destroyer Hammann was alongside, attempting to provide power for the salvage team. At this point the Japanese submarine I.168 fired two torpedoes into the Yorktown and another into the Hammann which sank with heavy loss of life. The Yorktown had to be abandoned again. She remained afloat throughout the night only to sink at dawn the following day.

As in the case of HMS Ark Royal, torpedoed in the Mediterranean a year earlier, it is now felt that, had the salvage teams made more

Fleet Admiral Isoruku Yamamoto, commander in chief of the Japanese Imperial Navy, and the man who planned the attack on Pearl Harbor. He was overall commander of the Japanese operation against Midway and led one of the greatest naval forces ever assembled at that time, comprising eighty surface warships. However, he seems to have left too much to the Japanese carrier force and, when decisions had to be made, was uncharacteristically indecisive. Less than a year later he was killed when U.S. fighters from Guadalcanal shot up his transport aircraft at Bougainville.

effective use of counterflooding, the USS *Yorktown* might have been saved. However, this is precisely the kind of knowledge gained with hindsight and greater experience.

As a footnote to Midway: on 18 April, 1943, Admiral Isoruku Yamamoto, Commander in Chief of the Combined Japanese Fleet, was killed as his aircraft landed at Bougainville airfield. Intelligence decrypts had alerted the Americans to his visit, and his aircraft was shot down by U.S. P.38s from Guadalcanal.

CONVOY PQ17

Escort vessels riding out a gale near Iceland, where winds could gust to a hurricane force of over 100 m.p.h., causing damage to ships. Convoy PQ17 sailed for Russia from Iceland on 27 June, 1942, with a strong close escort and also considerable supporting forces at sea. Allied intelligence reports suggested that he German battleship *Tirpitz* and other surface ships were planning an attack.

Every senior commander taking a decision in wartime must be aware that many lives hang on his action. On 4 July, 1942, Britain's First Sea Lord took a decision in London which led to the sinking of twenty-four Allied merchant ships, and the deaths of most of their crews.

Admiral Sir Dudley Pound, and his advisers at the Admiralty, were responsible for ordering the escorts of Arctic convoy PQ17 to withdraw, and for instructing the merchant ships to scatter. Two thirds of the ships were sunk; only eleven got through.

A convoy disaster of this kind had been a long time coming, but was always inevitable, in one form or another. The special tragedy in this case was that it need not have happened at all.

The PQ series of convoys carrying supplies to the USSR began in late September, 1941. The ten ships of PQ1 sailed through safely with a cargo of war materials. At first, the Russian convoys seemed to lead a charmed life. It was not till PQ7 that the freighter *Waziristan* was torpedoed by U-134 while in convoy on 2 January, 1942.

By then it was becoming clear to the Germans just how important these convoys were to the Soviet forces fighting the German Army. They also realised that what had begun as a trickle of supplies was becoming a flood.

Churchill and Roosevelt had undertaken to supply the Russians each month with some 400 planes, 500 tanks and large quantities of rubber, aluminium and machine tools. Most of these goods, along with food and medical supplies, were being sent by sea to the northern

Russian ports of Archangel and Murmansk.

In January 1942 Hitler moved his newest and biggest battleship, the 43,000-ton *Tirpitz*, to Trondheim, about halfway up the Norwegian coast. Trondheim, lying at the end of a narrow fjord, had been chosen for the protection it offered from carrier-borne torpedo aircraft. It also came within the extreme range of bombers flying from Britain.

When the *Tirpitz* was joined at Trondheim by the *Admiral Scheer* and the *Prinz Eugen*, Admiral Tovey, commander in chief of the British Home Fleet, began to worry. Two more big ships, the *Lutzow* and the *Admiral Hipper*, were even further north in Narvik. This concentration was in part occasioned by Hitler's belief that the British would attack first in Norway.

No such British offensive was planned, but the presence of these powerful German surface forces in the area had to be taken seriously. The German ships might raid out into the Atlantic or, more likely, make surface attacks on the Russian convoys. Either way they constituted that naval threat 'a fleet in being', which meant that Tovey had to keep his main forces ready to act whatever move the Germans made.

Tovey's forces were considerable. In the immediate covering force for convoys, under Vice Admiral Curteis, he had a battleship, HMS *Duke of York*; a battlecruiser, HMS *Renown*; a cruiser and six destroyers. In his main body he had another battleship, HMS *King George V*; an aircraft carrier, HMS *Victorious*; a cruiser and another six destroyers. Unlike the Germans', his ships were operating a long way from their home base, without land-based aircraft cover.

If they were not blessed with covering storms, the alternative problem that the convoys to Russia might face was too great a visibility. At that latitude, summer meant nights of almost perpetual daylight. U-boats and German aircraft had almost twenty-four hours every day in which to locate a convoy, and either attack it themselves or shadow it and continually report its position.

An escort vessel bringing up the rear of a convoy, which is keeping station admirably. In heavy seas, and with ships of varying kinds in any one convoy, this was not always easy. An escort commander often had to decide whether to detach a warship to keep company with a single dropout, or to keep his force together to face a main attack.

The Germans seemed to hold most of the aces. They could decide when to take the initiative and where to ambush the convoys. In winter the merchantmen steamed within easy reach of the German bases in Norway when pack ice prevented then swinging farther north. Land-based *Luftwaffe* aircraft could cover the German ships and also act as a strike force while the U-boats could shadow the convoys and lay a cordon across their route to Russia.

The only inhibiting factors were, firstly, Hitler's order not to attack until it was clear there was no danger of attack from Allied carrier-borne aircraft and, as always, the weather. When the *Tirpitz* made her first reconnaissance in force, in search of convoy PQ12, she ran into a full gale, encountering tempestuous seas, snow squalls and, a particularly unpleasant feature of midwinter sailing in that area, 'sea-smoke', a kind of blinding Arctic fog.

Although the *Tirpitz* narrowly missed homeward-bound convoy QP8, the weather prevented any other contact. PQ12 and the homeward-bound ships from Murmansk actually sailed right through each other in the worst sea-smoke fog of 1942 without realising they had done so.

The nineteen ships of the next convoy, PQ13, set sail on 20 March. Ten U-boats were waiting for it, and QP9 sailing in the opposite direction. Once again the main enemy was the appalling weather conditions. The convoy was dispersed by gales, and five stragglers or vessels separated from their escorts were lost to U-boats or German destroyers.

Destroyer Z-26 and U-585 were sunk, but the cruiser HMS *Trinidad* was hit by one of her own torpedoes, and would be lost on the way back.

PQ14 and PQ15 fared a little better, both in terms of the weather, which worked to their advantage, and in escaping most of the enemy's attentions. Nevertheless, the convoy commodore of PQ14 was lost aboard the *Empire Howard*, as were several ships from the returning convoy QP10.

PQ16 took something of a hammering,

losing several ships together with their valuable cargoes. On 2 May, 1942, the cruiser HMS *Edinburgh* was torpedoed by U-456, and had to be sunk. A small quantity of gold bullion she was carrying to Russia went down with her.

One should never forget the normal hazards of operating at sea. On 1 May, 1942, the destroyer HMS *Punjabi* was in collision with the battleship *King George V*. As she sank, her depth charges exploded and damaged the battleship. On 2 May the Polish submarine *Jastrzab*, off her official course, was attacked by Allied forces, and eventually sunk.

With two cruisers sunk and steadily losing their merchant ships, the Allies seriously began to question the sense of trying to send convoys during the rest of the summer, when there was almost perpetual daylight in the Arctic. However, Stalin was adamant that the supplies should continue to arrive. It was now clear to him that he could not rely on the opening of a second front in Europe to relieve pressure on his forces.

Reluctantly, the British Admiralty accepted that political necessity outweighed the strategic considerations. PQ17 would sail from Iceland as planned on 27 June, 1942, and hope to fight her way past the U-boats and dive bombers as best she could.

In addition to her close escort of six destroyers, four corvettes, two anti-aircraft ships, two submarines and seven smaller vessels, the supporting escort force would also be considerably stronger. It would consist of four 8-inch gun cruisers, HMS *Norfolk*, HMS *London*, USS *Wichita* and USS *Tuscaloosa*, together with three more destroyers. This cruiser force was commanded by British Rear Admiral Louis Hamilton, flying his flag in the *Norfolk*. The close escort was commanded by Commander 'Jackie' Broome on board HMS *Keppel*.

In the background, acting as a distant escort, and prepared to come in if the *Tirpitz* appeared, was Tovey's force, comprising two modern battleships, HMS *Duke of York* and USS *Washington*, an aircraft carrier, two cruisers and nine, later fourteen, destroyers. Nevertheless the initiative still lay with the Germans.

For seven days, the thirty-six merchant ships of convoy PQ17 steamed through the almost perpetual daylight of a northern summer day unhindered. Allied intelligence knew that the Germans were after the convoy. Indeed, German intelligence had been tracking it almost since the moment it sailed, and at least two U-boats were now shadowing it. Eight other U-boats were directed towards it or positioned to establish a patrol line in its direct path.

Then the German surface ships began to move. The two pocket battleships, the *Admiral Scheer* and the *Lutzow*, and six destroyers were ordered north from Narvik to Altafjord. Then the *Tirpitz* and the *Hipper* also left Trondheim and headed north. It was clear from intercepted signals and aircraft reports that PQ17 was under real threat.

Whether their long period of inactivity was to blame, or simply the bad weather, the German ships did not manage an orderly departure. Three destroyers escorting the *Tirpitz* ran onto rocks, and the unlucky *Lutzow* also ran aground, putting her out of the operation altogether.

Ultimate control of PQ17 was being exercised from the Admiralty in London, where every report and intercepted message was scrutinised and evaluated very carefully. On the evening of 4 July, Admiral Sir Dudley Pound decided he could not afford to have the supporting force of four 8-inch cruisers, of which two were a double responsibility, being Americans under command, smashed by the formidable German 15-inch, 11-inch and 7-inch guns assembled against them. The recent losses of both the *Edinburgh* and the *Trinidad* on the convoys made Pound even more cautious. He took the decision to order the escorting warships to withdraw and the convoy to scatter.

The order was received with utter dismay by Rear Admiral Hamilton of the supporting escort. Commander Broome of the close escort, to whose destroyers the order for withdrawal also applied, shared Hamilton's feelings. Admiral Tovey was not consulted; he was anyway not privy to the ULTRA intelligence reports that were flowing into the Admiralty, and on which Pound was basing his decision.

The naval escorts watched the dispersal of PQ17 with sadness: it seemed as though their lambs were being thrown to the wolves. Numerous accounts stress the grief and fury of the navy men ordered to abandon their responsibilities at the very moment they were

The battlecruiser HMS *Renown* was part of one of several naval forces at sea in support of Convoy PQ17. In addition to the close escort of destroyers and corvettes, there was a cruiser squadron, comprising two British and two U.S. 8-inch gun cruisers, and an immediate covering force under Vice Admiral Curteis, consisting of a modern battleship, the battlecruiser HMS *Renown*, a cruiser and six destroyers. Although the *Renown* was built in 1916, she was very seaworthy, well armoured and carried six 15-inch guns.

preparing to defend the convoy.

Of course they would have been heavily outgunned if all the German warships had appeared. However previous battles, such as the River Plate, had shown that well-handled cruisers could give a very good account of themselves.

The decision was not only wrong, but absolutely unnecessary. The *Tirpitz* did not even put to sea until after the U-boats had signalled the escorts' departure and the convoy's dispersal. In effect, a convoy was sacrificed and the Royal Navy ordered to make an ignominious withdrawal almost in the face of the enemy, simply because a German battleship moved her anchorage from one Norwegian fjord to another.

What will never be known is what would have happened if the two escorting groups had tried to fight the convoy through, or even if the destroyers of the close escort alone had stayed with the merchantmen and tried to save them from the U-boats.

After the convoy scattered, U-boats and squadrons of different German aircraft picked them off one by one, almost at will. In Arctic waters, even in midsummer, there was not much hope for crews when their ships sank.

Captain Broome, as he had become, won a healthy sum in damages for libel as a result of a suggestion that his withdrawal of the close-escort destroyers was a cowardly one. Nevertheless it has never stopped people speculating as to what might have happened if either Broome or Rear Admiral Hamilton had turned a blind eye to that Admiralty signal ordering them to withdraw.

The scattering of a convoy was not a simple *sauve qui peut* race off into the blue by each individual merchantman. It was meant to be a carefully orchestrated manoeuvre, as laid down in convoy regulations. Each ship was supposed to take on a different compass bearing to make it that much harder for any surface attacker or attackers to concentrate on more than a small proportion of the ships at any one time.

This had worked in the autumn of 1941 when the *Admiral Scheer* intercepted the Atlantic convoy escorted by the armed merchant cruiser HMS *Jervis Bay*. While the *Jervis Bay* sacrificed herself, going down heroically to the 11-inch guns of the pocket battleship, her convoy scattered and most of

An ammunition-carrying ship in a convoy carrying lend-lease supplies to Russia suffers a direct hit. The date is September 1942 and the attack took place within the Arctic circle far to the north of Norway. The courage of seamen willing to sail in ships carrying explosives or in tankers laden with gasolene cannot be underestimated, especially in these northern waters where survival times in the water were measured in minutes.

the ships survived.

If PQ17 had been massacred by the *Tirpitz* and her cohorts, both the supporting escort and Broome's close escort would probably have gone down too. Had they disobeyed the order to withdraw, an order given by those who knew the whole picture, they might have hazarded all future convoy operations to Russia. They might have lost more than just the one engagement they did, by losing the whole force of cruisers and destroyers that would make later journeys possible.

The destruction of PQ17 did lead to a pause in the convoys to Russia. Only when the nights grew darker again in the fall did they resume.

PQ18 fought its way through in September, but lost thirteen out of its forty-six ships in the process. However, the circumstances were not the same. PQ18's escort had been reinforced by an anti-aircraft cruiser and by the escort

carrier HMS *Avenger*, with twelve Sea Hurricanes aboard.

This escort gave a good account of itself, sinking three U-boats, including two of those which had sunk ships from PQ17, and shooting down more than thirty German torpedo-bombers and other aircraft. PQ18 was the last of the big convoys, the next tactic would be to run smaller groups with even larger escorts; but PQ19 belongs to another battle.

PQ17 is the convoy that will always be remembered. Sadly it goes down in history not in a blaze of glory, but simply as an example of where a distant headquarters overrode the men on the spot, and got it wrong. There will always remain that lingering doubt as to what might have happened if the Admiralty orders had been ignored and the convoy had fought on.

BATTLE OF THE BARENTS SEA

The Barents Sea is a part of the Arctic Ocean lying at the very northern tip of Europe. Its limits are, roughly, the Norwegian island of Spitzbergen, the Russian island of Novaya Zemlya and Lappland on the mainland. The sea is named after the sixteenth-century Dutch navigator Willem Barents, who had sought a northeast sea passage to Asia.

Through it steamed the Allied merchantmen on the last lap of their journies to Russia, taking those essential supplies promised by Roosevelt and Churchill to Stalin. In summer they could sail into the White Sea to Archangel. In winter, when the White Sea froze, their journey generally ended at Murmansk on the Kola peninsula.

As has been described above, the North Russia PQ convoys went through virtually unscathed, except by the weather, for the first few months. Up to March 1942, only one ship out of the 110 sailing this convoy route had been lost. Then that summer came the disastrous PQ17 convoy, which lost more than two thirds of its thirty-three ships, and this was followed by PQ18, which fared slightly better, but still lost thirteen out of forty-six.

By this time it was clear that the Germans were determined to cut this Russian supply line, using U-boats, aircraft, and surface ships.

As the winter weather worsened in late 1942, and although the Arctic nights at least became darker, the British Admiralty decided to split these convoys to North Russia into smaller fleets. They increased the numbers of escorts and sent more powerful supporting naval forces to hover in the background.

The biggest problem for these convoys was that when they reached the North Cape, that northernmost tip of Norway, they had to go through a sea passage only 250 miles wide. Arctic ice stopped them swinging further north, away from the German bases in the Norwegian fjords.

What would have been convoy PQ19 was secretly renumbered JW51 for security reasons, and then split into two parts as JW51A and JW51B.

Once again, Hitler took political decisions, based on his own hunches, which would only complicate an otherwise straightforward naval situation. The German leader was convinced that Churchill planned to attack Norway. This was his main reason for bringing his powerful surface ships to the area. Unwisely, he also withdrew a fairly large number of U-boats from their much more useful work in the Atlantic.

In fact, apart from occasional commando raids, all the Allied effort was going into Operation Torch, the November 1942 landings by British and American troops at Algiers, Casablanca and Oran in North Africa.

However, the supplies reaching Russia were important, and Hitler now had the ships, U-boats and aircraft in Norway to do something about them. It was also time for his largely inactive surface forces to earn their keep and prove to cynics like Goering that a continuing investment in ships for the German Navy was worthwhile.

Vice Admiral O. Kummetz, flying his flag in the 8-inch gun cruiser *Admiral Hipper*, under Captain Hans Hartmann, was ready in Altenfjord, north of Narvik. The force also included the pocket-battleship *Lutzow*, under Captain R. Stange, with its six 11-inch guns, and six destroyers.

Without prejudging events, it is fair to say that the German forces entered the Battle of the Barents Sea with one hand tied behind their backs. It was known that Hitler could not bear to lose any more of his bigger ships, despite what they might achieve against the enemy in battle.

Consequently, instructions from Admiral Kluber, Flag Officer, Northern Waters to Admiral Kummetz included: 'Procedure on meeting the enemy: avoid a superior force, but otherwise destroy convoy PQ20'. The Germans still thought of the two halves of convoy JW51 as PQ19 and PQ20.

By this time the sixteen merchant ships of JW51A had got through to Russia without being attacked. Their supporting force consisted of two British cruisers, HMS *Sheffield* and HMS *Jamaica*, and two destroyers. The cruisers were able to anchor and enjoy a Christmas break in Varenga Bay, off the Kola inlet, before sailing out again, to meet JW51B.

The fourteen ships of convoy JW51B, were following on the same course, but a week behind. They assembled in Loch Ewe on the far west coast of the Scottish Highlands, and set sail on 22 December, 1942. Four of the fourteen merchantmen were British, nine were American, and the remaining one was Panamanian. The

Hitler reviews the reborn German Fleet in 1936. The fleet comprised more than one hundred vessels, including three pocket battleships, nineteen submarines and cruisers and destroyers. With him is Admiral Raeder and the Minister of War, Werner von Blomberg. From this moment on Hitler played an active part in directing the war at sea, until he lost patience with the Navy and its admirals after their defeat in the Battle of the Barents Sea.

Right: German
torpedo planes in an
attack on an Allied
convoy in the Barents
Sea. Convoys were
particularly exposed
as they rounded the
North Cape on the
last leg of their
journey to Murmansk.

German dive
bombers (left) based
in Norway were a
major threat to the
Russian convoys.
Junkers 88s, such as
these, wreaked havoc
on the ships of
convoy PQ17, but bad
weather and the
presence of German
warships prevented
the Stukas playing
any significant part in
the Battle of the
Barents Sea.

British convoy commodore was aboard the *Empire Archer*; the vice commodore was the American master of the Panamanian *Calobre*. The close escort, as was usual on these Russian convoys, was all British. It was led by HMS *Onslow* and consisted of six other destroyers, a minesweeper, two corvettes, and two trawlers.

The Germans had codenamed their attack on JW51B Operation Rainbow (*Regenbogen*). It was bad enough that they had been told to avoid a superior force, a thing an inferior force might not always be able to do, but the pocket battleship *Lutzow* was under further pressure, scheduled as she was, to go on afterwards and act as a raider in the Atlantic. Her captain was obviously keen to avoid any battle damage that might handicap this raiding.

Things would get worse. Admiral Raeder appears to have passed Hitler's qualms about losing ships on down the chain of command. Admiral Carls, who commanded 'Group North' from Kiel in Germany, passed responsibility to Admiral Kluber in Norway, who sent a signal to Admiral Kummetz in charge of Operation Rainbow. This signal further complicated the earlier order about avoiding a superior force. Kummetz was now instructed: 'In spite of operational orders, exercise restraint if you contact enemy of comparable strength, since it is undesirable to run excessive risks to the cruisers'. This is no way to send a naval force into battle.

However, with a few minor hiccups, again resulting from their long period of inactivity, the German naval force put to sea on 30 December, 1942. JW51B had already been spotted by a *Luftwaffe* reconnaisance aircraft and was being shadowed by U-354. The two British cruisers, HMS *Sheffield* and HMS *Jamaica*, were now on their way back from Russia to join this convoy. They were to sweep round the merchant ships and prevent any attack on these by German warships from the rear. The usual supporting distant cover consisted of a battleship, HMS *Anson*, flying the flag of Vice Admiral Fraser, a heavy cruiser and three destroyers, with four submarines on call.

Rear Admiral Robert L. Burnett, on HMS *Sheffield*, had guessed correctly. The Germans did plan to attack from the rear, and they split their force to do so. This would normally be bad tactics, as it gives the enemy a chance to deal with each section in turn. In this case, it might have worked but for the determination of the *Lutzow*'s captain to avoid any damage that would handicap her as a raider.

The first contact came at about 0830 hours on 31 December, 1942. A corvette from the convoy's close escort saw some German destroyers, but did not report them. She guessed that they were Russian vessels come out to escort the convoy on its last stage to Murmansk. This guess was understandable, but wrong.

Ten minutes later the German destroyers were spotted by HMS *Obdurate* and reported to Captain Robert St.Vincent Sherbrooke DSO on HMS *Onslow*. The *Obdurate* was ordered to investigate, and soon found herself within four miles of the Germans, who opened fire.

Captain Sherbrooke put his planned defence strategy into action. His main force of 'O' Class destroyers would go straight for the enemy, whilst the destroyer HMS *Achates* and three smaller vessels laid a smoke screen to protect the convoy.

HMS *Onslow*, followed by HMS *Obedient* and HMS *Orwell*, raced to support the *Obdurate*. By then the *Admiral Hipper* herself was within range, and firing at the smoke-screen-laying *Achates*. The *Onslow* and the *Orwell* immediately engaged the German cruiser, and also made as though to attack with torpedoes. The *Obdurate* and the *Obedient* doubled back to stop the *Hipper*'s accompanying destroyers attacking the convoy.

Bad light at first affected the *Hipper*'s accuracy, but it soon improved. HMS *Onslow* was badly hit, and fires started. The escort commander, Captain Sherbrooke, was seriously wounded. Command passed to the next senior officer, Lt Commander D.C. Kinloch in the *Obedient*. Shortly afterwards the *Hipper* disappeared into a snow flurry.

The two British cruisers, the *Sheffield* and the *Jamaica* had finally reached the area. They had been delayed by meeting a British trawler, escorting a merchantman that had become detached from the convoy, and had found it almost impossible to decide which ships were which.

The 875-ton minesweeping sloop HMS *Bramble*, had also become detached from the convoy during a storm. She suddenly appeared close to the *Hipper* and her three destroyers, and was annihilated by German guns. None of her crew of 120 survived.

Meanwhile, the *Lutzow* and her three accompanying destroyers had found the convoy and was all set to destroy it when a squall obscured this sitting duck of a target. The *Lutzow* decided to wait for the weather to clear!

The British destroyers, now back with the convoy, manoeuvred to keep between it and the *Lutzow*, and laid more smoke. Then the *Hipper* attacked from a different direction and badly damaged HMS *Achates*. Despite coming under heavy fire, the British destroyers swung round again to threaten the *Hipper* with their torpedoes. Suddenly, the *Sheffield* and the *Jamaica* were in the battle. They scored hits on the *Hipper* with their combined force of twenty-four 6-inch guns, at a range of 14,000 yards. The *Hipper*'s damage reduced her speed to 28 knots, from a maximum of 32.

Admiral Kummetz decided to withdraw. Before they could do so, two German destroyers came within 4,000 yards of the British cruisers. One destroyer, the *Friedrick Eckoldt*, was reduced to a burning wreck, the other escaped into a snow squall that also hid the *Hipper*.

The split-force tactics now began to work to the Germans' advantage. The *Lutzow* was back on the attack again, though at the safe range of 18,000 yards. She damaged a merchant ship before the three surviving British destroyers could swing towards her, again laying smoke.

No sooner had the *Lutzow* ceased fire, than the *Hipper* reappeared, bringing accurate guns to bear on the destroyers. Luckily, the German admiral once again ordered a withdrawal. The destroyers went back to the convoy, where HMS *Achates* was now sinking.

Although the picture is somewhat posed, it provides a good example of the precautions necessary on a Russia-bound convoy. A U.S. naval gunner sporting a bearskin duffel coat mans a defensive gun on the stern of a merchant ship on the Murmansk run.

There was a final clash between the *Hipper* and the two British cruisers, in which neither side scored any hits, and, some four hours after it had begun, the Battle of the Barents Sea was over.

The British lost a destroyer and a minesweeper, and suffered damage to other ships. The Germans lost a destroyer, and the *Hipper* was damaged. Although repaired, she was never used in operations again.

It was not a large battle, but it was a significant one. The British destroyers, by going baldheaded for the enemy every time, achieved their purpose of protecting their convoy. This arrived in Russia safe and on time; an example of what might have been done for PQ17. For his planning and leadership in the first hour of combat, Captain Sherbrooke was awarded the Victoria Cross. Like Nelson, he lost the sight of an eye, but still became an admiral.

The two supporting British cruisers under Admiral Burnett, the *Sheffield* and the *Jamaica*, had ultimately been there when they were needed, though Admiral Burnett was criticised for the time it took for them to arrive. Basically, however, this was a classic destroyer battle, in which the threat to use torpedoes against bigger ships proved very effective.

The Germans, only partly due to the rigid orders from their Admiralty, were surprisingly unaggressive. The *Lutzow* and her destroyers seem to have been particularly timid. Ironically, having successfully preserved herself for raiding, the *Lutzow's* sortie into the Atlantic was then cancelled.

The Battle of the Barents Sea proved a number of things. Above all, it showed the danger of sending a naval force into action with restrictive orders decided in advance and leaving the commander on the spot little opportunity to exercise his own judgement. In the case of the *Lutzow* it highlighted the danger

German naval officers discussing operational plans aboard a German warship. The failure of Operation Rainbow in the Barents Sea infuriated Hitler and led to Admiral Raeder resigning.

of giving a ship two separate missions: both to attack a convoy and to preserve oneself for distance raiding.

However, it was only after the War that the full extent of what the Battle of the Barents Sea had achieved became known. Hitler was so incensed by this further failure of his Navy that he declared the ships should be paid off and their crews used elsewhere in the war effort. Admiral Raeder resigned in response to Hitler's fury and U-boat chief Admiral Donitz was appointed to succeed him.

Even had the British been aware of this possible outcome, they could probably not have done better or been braver.

German naval officers discussing operational plans aboard a German warship. The failure of Operation Rainbow in the Barents Sea infuriated Hitler and led to Admiral Raeder resigning.

SUBMARINES

A submarine was simply one long corridor, and the engine room (left) was perhaps its narrowest part. The smell of fuel was ever present, and there were no quiet corners. Communal living was a necessary way of life, as there were probably only enough bunks to sleep half the crew at any one time. A single lavatory would be shared by thirty to forty men, and there was no chance of a shower for the length of the patrol. On British submarines, the practice was to have the main meal of the day (right) at midnight.

There is something about submarines that captures the imagination. This is shown by the multitude of books, films and television programmes on the subject. It is also demonstrated in the exciting accounts of their exploits given by individual submarine commanders.

Submarine crews are often depicted as a small band of brothers, operating in distant waters with every man's hand against them. Their camaraderie and a little of the stress under which they sailed makes for a good story and for 'good viewing'.

The reality was much tougher. Submarine crews operated under permanently atrocious conditions, and were often in continual danger. They had to contend with all the hazards of the weather in a small, cramped vessel, in which comfort was a minor consideration.

The stale air of the submarine was thick with the permanent stench of fuel, sweat and, more pleasantly, cooking smells. In most of the smaller wartime boats there were not enough bunks to go round, so these were in permanent use by whichever watch was not on duty. The whole vessel was a corridor, with no privacy and no quiet. The crew of forty to sixty officers and men generally had to share a single lavatory.

Above all, was the thought that, when attacked by destroyers with depth charges, there was a distinct likelihood of being sunk with no chance of escape. U-boats were sardonically known by their crews as 'Iron coffins'. Yet the submarine services never

Top left: the USS *Grampus* at sea in the early days of the war. Most British and U.S. submarines were given names as well as numbers, and these names were often those of fish or marine animals. The grampus is a spouting blunt-headed dolphin-like cetacean, and there was a submarine with this name in both the British and US Navies.

Bottom left: the control room of a U.S. submarine below the surface. While one officer is ready to use the periscope, another is supervising the motor control. A gauge indicates the submarine is at forty feet.

The need for vigilance whenever a submarine surfaced was paramount, even on a training patrol (right). Generally submarines surfaced at night to recharge their batteries and let some fresh air get in below. They always had to be ready to dive at once if enemy surface vessels or aircraft appeared.

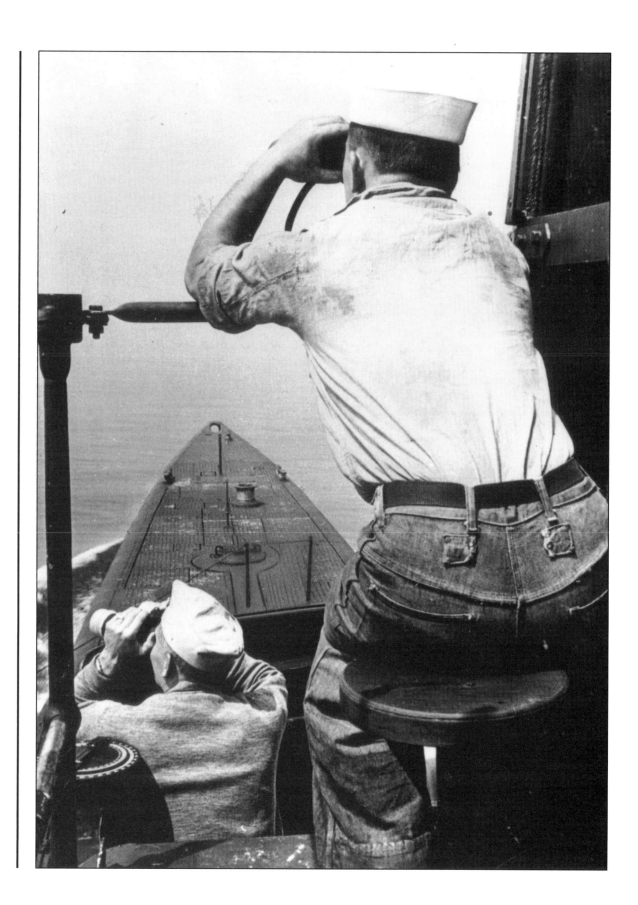

seemed to lack willing crewmen.

The concept of volunteering may well have varied from navy to navy, wartime and patriotic pressures being what they are. However, no submarine would have survived if anything more than the occasional individual had been a reluctant 'pressed man'.

The role of the submarine in the battle at sea kept changing. In World War I submarines were initially seen as outriders to the fleet, serving partly as underwater spies and partly as something akin to a mobile mine. The British saw them as a particularly dangerous and underhand form of naval warfare. They suspected most German surface manoeuvres were designed to lead the Royal Navy into submarine traps.

Later in the First World War, German U-boats proved very effective as undersea raiders. They nearly succeeded in bringing Great Britain to her knees by their attacks on her shipping. In April 1917, enemy action, predominantly that of U-boats, sank 880,000 tons of Allied shipping. Most of this was carrying vital supplies, including food, to Britain.

When World War II began, the British started with surface naval forces greatly superior to those of the German *Kriegsmarine*. The potential value of the *Luftwaffe* against ships at sea, particularly those far out in the Atlantic, was unknown. Only the U-boats were seen as likely to sever or interrupt Britain's supply lines from overseas, and there were comparatively few of them available in 1939.

Despite all the lessons supposedly learned in World War I, and despite all the new technological advances for dealing with the U-boat problem, the German submarines came very close to achieving their objective.

Save for the intervention of the politicians, Admiral Donitz might have won the Battle of the Atlantic very early in the War. However, in the summer of 1941, Hitler gave orders for six U-boats to be sent to the Mediterranean; these were followed by a further six.

Rommel was doing well against the British in the desert, but his supplies from Italy were under constant attack from the Royal Navy. Hitler and Mussolini controlled the whole of the northern coastline of the Mediterranean. However, the British had naval bases at either end, in Gibraltar and at Alexandria, in Egypt,

Loading torpedoes on board a German U-boat. The most common submarine, the Type VII, had five torpedo tubes – four in front and one in the stern. 730 Type VII U-boats were commissioned during the course of the War, of which over 550 were sunk or otherwise lost.

A U.S. submarine taking on ammunition for its 5-inch deck gun before going out on patrol. It was mainly American submarines built for the Pacific that carried a 5-inch gun; most British and German guns were 4-inch or smaller. Of the seventy-three Gato-class submarines completed between 1942 and 1944, nineteen were sunk on active service.

and also the island fortress of Malta in the middle.

Hitler wanted the U-boats to help a reinforced *Luftwaffe* protect the supply lines to Africa by sinking British warships. The first six U-boats hardly accomplished anything. Two of the second group did not reach the Mediterranean, and a third was sunk soon after.

Nevertheless, in November 1941 U-boats scored two important successes. The aircraft carrier HMS *Ark Royal* and the battleship HMS *Barham* were both sunk, with heavy loss of life

in the latter case. An Australian destroyer, HMAS *Paramatta,* was also sunk.

In effect, Hitler's diversion of twelve U-boats to the Mediterranean gave Allied shipping in the Atlantic a two-month 'holiday', at a time when they badly needed one. As 1941 came to an end, Britain was well stocked up with supplies and in a stronger psychological position to continue waging the battle of the Atlantic.

It would be nice to think that everything that was learned about employing submarines in the Atlantic and in the Mediterranean was

immediately transferred to the Allied forces in the Pacific. This was not so, partly because of a traditional reluctance of any navy to learn from another, and also because the war in the Pacific would prove so different, in particular in the role of the submarine.

Despite this need to repeat a learning curve, it has been said that in the Pacific the United States turned the submarine into 'one of the most successful weapons of the war'. By the autumn of 1944, they had torn the bottom out of the Japanese merchant fleet, and by the end of the War had sunk 5,500,000 tons of enemy shipping.

Somehow the Japanese never succeeded in using submarines in the same way as their German partners. They insisted on building some of the largest submarines in the world, but the quality of these in terms of design and performance was poor. They certainly achieved some successes, for example when I.168 at Midway used its torpedoes to finish off the U.S. aircraft carrier *Yorktown* and sink the destroyer *Hammann*. Yet even at Midway they failed in their main task, which was to prevent the American carrier force coming through their cordon undetected.

Thanks to superior intelligence, the two American carrier task forces reached a hidden position north of Midway before the Japanese submarine cordon was in place east of the island. It was Japanese staff work aboard submarines that failed at Midway, not the submarines. Their overall commander had not been at the planning war games, nor did he issue detailed orders to his submariners.

Did the Japanese failure, or their general lack of success, with submarines stem from the 'big ship' attitude cultivated by officers of the Imperial Japanese Navy? Or were the Japanese temperamentally unsuited to the kind of all-ranks camaraderie and integration and, above all, initiative that was needed?

By the end of the War, Japanese submarines were mainly being used for long-range reconnaissance, or even as supply transports and troop carriers, rather than as an offensive weapon against the huge Allied amphibious and naval forces by then filling Pacific waters.

The American submarine commanders in the Pacific, on the other hand, included some of the very best men in the U.S. Navy. They do seem to have inspired levels of team spirit and a tenacious courage that were both unique and vitally necessary on patrols that were long by any submariner's standards. They also developed their own tactics, one of the most successful being hunting in pairs. It would be

the USS *Darter* and USS *Dace* which first reported the main Japanese striking force heading for the Leyte Gulf, and who then each took the opportunity to sink a Japanese cruiser.

Submarine warfare in the east followed much the same pattern as surface warfare there. When the Imperial Japanese Navy reigned supreme, and swept through the Indian Ocean as far as Ceylon, Japanese and German submarines operated freely. There was a burst of activity in the first three months of 1944, during which one of their victims was the transport *Khedive Ismail*, which sank with the loss of 1,300 lives, including those of many servicewomen and nurses.

After this, slowly but surely, the Axis submarine retreat began, much in the same way as progress was made against Japan's surface ships.

The Allies began accounting for supply tankers and supply U-boats, and by 1944 British submarines were sinking enemy ships in waters off Malaya and Sumatra. United States submarines proved even more successful, and really began to dominate all the more northern Pacific waters. In March 1944, Japanese submarines ceased to operate from their base at Rabaul, and withdrew to Truk – even though the Japanese army continued to man Rabaul until 1945.

By mid-1945, well over eighty percent of all Japanese merchant shipping had been sunk, two thirds of the ships being lost to submarines. The noticeable decline in Allied submarine successes as the War went on was simply because there were no more ships to sink, and action was having to be directed against the small coastal craft and junks which the Japanese were now using.

By the end of the War, it was clear that the United States had mastered the art of submarine warfare in a way that not even the Germans had managed to do in their own Atlantic heyday. American submarines operated as an integral part of fleet operations, while succeeding equally well as wolf-pack raiders and individual marauders. They made a major contribution to victory in the Pacific.

The Japanese midget submarine "D", involved in the attack on Pearl Harbor in 1941, is raised (left) from near the harbour entrance in 1960 - nearly twenty years later. Thirty years on, no trace, as far as is known, has ever been found of its two-man crew. The reason for its loss is also still a mystery.

NORTH AFRICA AND SICILY

The Allied landings on 8 November, 1942, in North Africa, code-named Operation Torch, were the biggest amphibious operation undertaken anywhere at that stage of the War. The landings themselves were not strongly opposed by the Vichy French forces, which was just as well as both the U.S. and the British forces still had a lot to learn about attacking from the sea. The U.S. gun crew (right) are manhandling their weapon up the beach through the sand.

For eighteen months, between March 1941 and September 1942, Germany's General Rommel set the pace in the Western Desert of North Africa. He was undeniably one of the most able commanders of the Second World War. Rommel was a master of the almost fleet-like manoeuvering required of armoured forces for the open-desert warfare of Libya.

After capturing Tobruk in mid-1942, his *Panzers* had driven the British out of the rest of Libya and back into Egypt. However, his forces and his supply lines were now fully stretched, and the British 8th Army was well dug in at El Alamein. The salt marshes of the Qattara Depression acted as a barrier against Rommel's favourite outflanking manoeuvre.

The United States helped replace a high proportion of the British equipment lost at Tobruk. Amongst the supplies were a quantity of thirty-ton Sherman M.4 tanks and one hundred self-propelled guns. Britain's General Alexander, who was meant to be General Eisenhower's second in command for the coming North African landings, was 'borrowed back' to take over in Egypt.

Another British commander, General Bernard Montgomery, was also 'borrowed' from Eisenhower's team, to take over the 8th Army. He replaced General Gott, who had been killed in an air crash.

On the evening of 23 October, 1942, Montgomery's 8th Army attacked at El Alamein. After a fiercely contested battle, the 8th army began pushing the Germans and their Italian

In a scene more reminiscent of peacetime trooping, British troops disembark (left) from a transport after the capture of Algiers. From a naval point of view the most remarkable feature was the way in which vast convoys sailed to North Africa from both Britain and the United States, with the loss of only one ship.

After the landings much of the action in Algiers was political, with General Eisenhower engaged in persuading Marshal Pétain's representative, Admiral Darlan, to come in on the Allied side. General Eisenhower poses (top right) with Admiral Darlan and General Mark Clark. They are joined by Britain's Admiral Sir Andrew Cunningham (bottom right), whose naval forces did so much to dominate the Mediterranean. A month after the meeting, Admiral Darlan was killed by an assassin.

allies back into Libya. The tide had turned again, both in Africa and in the War as a whole.

An outline of progress in the Desert War is needed to set the scene for the battles we shall now consider: the amphibious landings in North Africa, Sicily and Italy. This was a new kind of battle at sea. Not since the ill-fated British and ANZAC expedition to Gallipoli in 1915 had any major amphibious warfare of this kind been part of Allied strategy in Europe.

A couple of months before El Alamein, and three months before the landings in Morocco and Algeria, a dreadful rehearsal was held. This was Operation Jubilee, an Anglo-Canadian attack on the French port of Dieppe across the English Channel. A full report on the events of 19 August, 1942, was not published until thirty years later and the action remains controversial to this day.

With hindsight it is fair to see Dieppe as an experiment, a practice landing or an invasion rehearsal, designed to see what could be achieved in a frontal assault on Germany's beach defences. It was also designed to discover the problems of a seaborne assault,

and to test the troops taking part. A suggestion that it was also a way of providing some action for Canadian troops, increasingly restless in boring wartime Britain, is not without credibility either.

Nobody likes to think of soldiers being used as guinea pigs. However, a large-scale raid of this kind was probably the only way to find out for certain what the pitfalls of an invasion were. The pitfalls were certainly found out, but the experiment was fatal for many of those involved.

The element of surprise was lost when the invading force encountered a German coastal convoy, though the Germans had anyway anticipated a raid of this kind. Two British Commando units and 6,000 troops from two Canadian infantry brigades took part, plus a small party of U.S. Rangers. Over 200 vessels were involved, including eight destroyers, nine Landing Ships, Infantry and 179 small landing craft.

Although one or two minor actions succeeded, the main assault did not. 1,179 men were killed, and 2,190 captured – over half the invaders. The Hunt class destroyer escort

The next amphibious landing after North Africa was in Sicily. An aerial view gives some impression of the scale of the operation needed to land an army on an enemy shore.

HMS *Berkeley* was lost, together with thirty-five landing craft and other vessels. None of the thirty tanks got off the beach, and over a hundred supporting aircraft were shot down. The Germans lost forty-eight aircraft and 311 troops.

Many valuable lessons learned at Dieppe were incorporated into Operation Torch, the Anglo-American landings in North Africa on 8 November, 1942. This invasion can also be seen as part of the learning process, as just about everything that could go wrong, did. The landing craft met strong winds and surf, and some parties were over five hours late in getting ashore. Dieppe and Operation Torch conclusively demonstrated that even 1943 was too soon for the kind of Second Front in Europe that the Russians were demanding.

On land, the Battle of El Alamein, which began on the night of 23/24 October, 1942, went well. The battle is accepted as a turning point in the War. Montgomery's troops began to force the enemy back into the Western Desert for the last time. The Operation Torch landings on the other side of North Africa would eventually trap the Germans in Tunisia, thus bringing the whole of North Africa under Allied control.

Operation Torch was the biggest amphibious operation undertaken to date. It involved organisation on a scale never before attempted by the U.S. Army and, despite many shortcomings, it worked.

The forces opposing the Allies were Vichy French, defending the North African territories of Morocco, Algeria and Tunisia. German forces would not be encountered till long after the landings had succeeded.

The first task of the naval forces was to get the troops safely to North Africa. Warships were expected to support the troops by bombardment and to stop any opposing forces from intervening. They were also responsible for the safe and punctual arrival of supplies and reinforcements, all of them coming by sea.

There were three main landings: by the Americans at Casablanca and Oran, and by the British near Algiers. The Vichy French were troops loyal to the government of Marshal Pétain, which ruled the unoccupied part of France and most of her overseas territories. Because of earlier incidents in North Africa between the British and the French, Operation Torch was publicly presented as very much an American affair. Some of the British officers involved at Casablanca and Oran even wore U.S. uniforms in order not to provoke French antipathy towards her former allies, who had since attacked the French Fleet. At Algiers, the British would go through the beachheads as quickly as possible to confront the Germans, who had by then occupied Tunisia.

The Allies won the first battle. This was to get the troopships through to their landing beaches safely. Considering the U-boat attacks on Atlantic convoys at this time this was a remarkable feat. Out of all the ships in the three giant convoys, only one was sunk. Eighty-one transports, the major part of the Torch invasion force, came from the British Isles. A further thirty-nine troopships, with an escort of forty-seven U.S. warships, sailed there directly from the other side of the Atlantic.

There was some spirited resistance from French naval forces, resulting in the loss of the cruiser *Primaguet*, ten destroyers and three submarines. The still unfinished French battleship *Jean Bart* in use as a floating fort at Casablanca, was put out of action by the U.S. battleship

Massachusetts.

It was all over fairly quickly. The Americans negotiated a ceasefire with Marshal Pétain's deputy, Admiral Darlan, who was on a visit to Algiers at the time of the landings. Three days later, on 11 November, 1942, the French surrendered.

There was still a lot of hard fighting ahead, both for the British forces driving across Libya from Egypt and for the Anglo-American forces who had landed on the other side, before the Germans and Italians in North Africa would surrender.

This first large-scale combined Allied operation and major amphibious invasion had worked. It demonstrated what could be achieved. The next amphibious invasion target was Sicily, planned for 10 July, 1943.

Accepting that they could not launch an invasion of northwest Europe until 1944, the Allies' strategy was to continue fighting in the south. Capturing Sicily would secure the Mediterranean's sea lines, and pave the way for an invasion of the Italian mainland thereafter. Invading Italy would necessitate the diversion of German forces from the Russian front. These would move to support their Italian allies and protect what Churchill always called the 'soft underbelly of Europe'. Italy originally had well over ninety army divisions. By this time roughly thirty of these had been destroyed or captured, another thirty were scattered around on garrison duty in the 'Axis Empire', and only the remaining thirty were at home in Italy itself.

Eisenhower's headquarters started planning the landings in Sicily long before Tunisia was won. Operation Husky, as it was called, was masterminded on the naval side by Admiral Ramsay. This British admiral had already organised the successful evacuation of Dunkirk in 1940, and was later to play a key role in the planning of D-day in June 1944.

The use of LSTs (Landing Ships, Tank) and LCTs (Landing Craft, Tank) provided the new dimension of armour going in with the first wave of infantry. Over a thousand ships were used to land eight divisions over a front of a hundred miles. By the evening of the second day, the Allies had 80,000 troops and 8,000 vehicles ashore – a truly fine piece of planning and organisation.

Sicily was no walkover, but the Allies had the necessary drive and the initiative. In one engagement, on the coast near Niscemi, the

Left: an Allied ship carrying ammunition explodes after being hit off Sicily. In all, during this first invasion of European territory, six ships were lost in the drive towards Rome and Berlin and the ultimate defeat of the Axis powers.

Right: some of the reinforcements arriving in Sicily came ashore fairly unhindered, in this case only getting their feet wet.

U.S. 1st Army Division, supported by the USS *Boise* and the USS *Savannah*, successfully bombarded the Hermann Goering *Panzerdivision*. It was the first occasion on which sea power decided a tank battle.

The main landing in Italy, on a large bay at Salerno, thirty miles southeast of Naples, was not easy. Operation Avalanche began on 9 September, 1943. It involved some fierce fighting and at times it was touch and go on individual Allied beachheads. However, naval and, in particular, air support ensured that the Allies were at last back on the continent of Europe, and that they were back to stay.

The campaign in Italy need concern us no further here, except, perhaps, to note that the Germans would reinforce their armies there considerably and would fight a stubborn rearguard action for the rest of the War.

After Italy sued for peace, and an armistice had been signed, at 5.15 p.m. on 3 September, 1943, exactly four years after the War began for the British, the Italian Fleet sailed for Malta to surrender. It was heavily bombed by its former allies, the Germans, and the battleship *Roma* was sunk with the loss of 1,500 lives – a sad end to a naval partnership, even if it had not been a very distinguished or successful one.

To complete the sequence of amphibious landings that constitute this chapter's battle at sea, we must mention just one more landing. This took place at Anzio on 22 January, 1944, and very nearly failed.

Overland progress northwards through Italy had been slow. A heavily reinforced German Army under Field Marshal Kesselring was fighting well, and the winter weather was atrocious. It was thought that the landing of an Allied force south of Rome at Anzio would ensure the early capture of the city, bypassing as it did the defences of the German Gustav Line.

Instead, the Allied forces were contained at Anzio and were very nearly thrown back into the sea. Hindsight lays much of the blame on the local commander of the British and U.S. troops involved, himself an American. As one historian described it, on finding that the Germans were not present in any strength, the

Allied troops finally fought their way back onto the continent of Europe via landings on the Italian mainland. Operation Avalanche at Salerno on 9 September, 1943, saw some fierce fighting and further losses among the landing forces. The cruiser USS *Savannah* (left) was hit by a bomb and had a turret knocked out of action.

Reinforcements at Salerno pass a wounded man being taken back on a stretcher. Note the steel mesh roadway laid down over the sand to allow trucks and guns to come ashore without difficulty.

general nevertheless behaved exactly as if they were. Having been told his priority was to establish a secure beachhead he did just that, spending eight days consolidating his position rather than striking out for Rome.

Rome would fall only two days before the launching of Operation Overlord, which was the biggest amphibious operation of the war in Europe and which began on 6 June, 1944.

BATTLE OF THE ATLANTIC

It was in the Battle of the Atlantic, which was a continuous battle throughout most of the years of both world wars, that the Allies came nearest each time to suffering defeat at sea. In both wars it was a battle Britain in particular could not afford to lose.

Britain, in its role as an 'unsinkable aircraft carrier', needed food and weapons from overseas if she was to survive. Much of this food, nearly all the raw materials to make guns and tanks, and even the weapons themselves, came from across the Atlantic.

Before the Second World War, Britain had the largest merchant navy in the world; one third of the total tonnage on the high seas was British. Now Hitler held most of the continent of Europe, including the entire coastline from the Arctic waters off the North Cape of Norway down to the Bay of Biscay and Spain. All the supplies destined for Britain had, therefore, to sail through the Atlantic in order to reach the United Kingdom. Some of the supplies would then go on to the Soviet Union, to sustain her too in the war against fascism.

In the Atlantic, and also on the route north to the Arctic ports of the USSR, the merchant ships and their escorts faced German surface raiders and U-boats. Furthermore, they had to battle against the weather, often as dangerous as the enemy itself.

In the Second World War the Battle of the Atlantic proper began with the defeat of France in July 1940, and the German occupation of the French west-coast ports of Brest, La Pallice, St. Nazaire, Lorient, and Bordeaux. The Battle of the Atlantic would continue for nearly six years, and would be fiercely fought, with the advantage continually passing from one side to the other.

The flag officer commanding the German U-boats, Admiral Donitz, moved his headquarters from Berlin to Lorient to be near his submarines. The U-boats would be Germany's main weapon in this battle for, after the sinking of the *Bismarck*, surface raiding in the Atlantic virtually ended. It nonetheless always remained a potential threat to the Arctic convoys.

For most of the War the main British headquarters for the Battle of the Atlantic were in Liverpool. From here the admiral in charge of the western approaches was responsible for the convoys and their escorts. With London's docks virtually closed by bombing and Britain's North Sea ports often endangered by mines, the ports on the west coast became the centre for most merchant shipping.

The importance of the battle was underlined by Churchill's setting-up of a special cabinet committee to meet the challenges to Britain's supply lifeline. A series of distinguished British admirals commanded the western approaches. These included such dignitaries as Sir Martin Dunbar-Nasmith, who won the Victoria Cross as a submariner in the Dardanelles in 1915, Sir Percy Noble and, perhaps the greatest of them all, Sir Max Horton. Each lobbied throughout his period in office for more resources for the vital Atlantic battle zone.

For, in addition to the actual fighting, this was to be a battle of resources. The Allies had to build ships faster than the German U-boats could sink them. They had to find escorts, and the crews to man them, in the face of dozens of other demands on the naval services. The air-force commanders had to be persuaded to divert much needed aircraft to Coastal Command rather than to the bombing campaign in Germany. The arguments, like the fighting out in the Atlantic, swayed back and forth, and with equal ferocity.

It is beyond the scope of this chapter to analyse the many occasions upon which policy or strategy influenced the course of the Battle of the Atlantic. John Terraine's account in *Business in Great Waters* is required reading for any serious student of the U-Boat wars.

It is, however, worth reminding ourselves of a few of the key factors. The assembly-line construction of all-welded American Liberty ships was crucial. These were coming on-stream so magnificently fast that they were keeping up with the losses being suffered at sea.

The provision of escorts was haphazard at times, and resulted in the use of a broad mix of vessels, manned by crews of very varying abilities. American assistance, even before the U.S.A. was involved in the War, was a determining factor. The provision of the fifty lend-lease destroyers in exchange for naval bases on British and Commonwealth territory was more than a token gesture. The repair

The key to winning the Battle of the Atlantic was air power. Whilst there was still a gap between the area which could be covered by U.S. Coast Guard aircraft (top right) and by the aircraft meeting convoys from airfields in Britain or Iceland, U-boats reigned supreme. Providing aircraft with a longer range became a priority for Allied chiefs, one that was eventually realised.

One extremely effective way of providing air cover for convoys was by using aircraft from escort carriers. Grumman Avengers (bottom right) could cover thousands of miles of sea in searching for threats to a convoy.

Left: a German U-boat under final attack from a long-range Liberator. Three U.S. Navy aircraft and two army bombers have successfully attacked the U-boat and smoke is coming from the conning tower. Strafing attacks have kept the U-boat crew from their guns. The circular splashes in the water mark cannon fire from the attacking plane.

facilities available in the U.S.A. were equally important.

For the Germans, the War had come too soon for the building plans which Donitz had counted on, and this meant that he always had less U-boats than he required. He started the War with only twenty-four U-boats ready for active service. Nevertheless, and despite RAF and U.S.AAF bombing, U-boat production never really faltered. Even in 1943 and 1944, the years of their greatest losses, U-boats were still being built faster than they were being sunk.

In strategic terms, the Allies' greatest missed opportunity was probably their failure to bomb the underground U-boat pens as these were being constructed. Once they were built, the pens provided an invulnerable haven for U-boats in port, for the Germans were masters in

the use of concrete. Losses in harbour were minimal for most of the War; U-boats had to be caught and sunk at sea.

Including some two dozen U-boats lost in collision or scuttled when Allied troops captured their home bases, out of the total 1,162 U-boats built, 791 were sunk in the Second World War.

After resources, politics also played its part in influencing the course of the Battle of the Atlantic. In the summer of 1941, Hitler took a decision which hindered Admiral Donitz's campaign against the supply ships travelling to Britain. He gave orders for six U-boats to go to the Mediterranean, to be followed by another six.

Rommel was doing well against the British in the desert, but his supplies from Italy were under constant attack from the Royal Navy.

A U-boat survivor is about to be taken aboard the Free French corvette *Aconit*. Note the breathing tube from the German seaman's escape gear around his neck. In an Atlantic convoy battle on 10 March, 1943, the *Aconit* helped sink both U-432 and U-444 either by gunfire or ramming.

Although Hitler and Mussolini controlled the whole of the northern coastline of the Mediterranean, the British had naval bases at either end, plus the beleaguered island fortress of Malta in the middle.

Hitler wanted these twelve U-boats to help a reinforced *Luftwaffe* protect the supply lines to Africa. The first six hardly accomplished anything. Two of the second group did not even reach the Mediterranean, and a third was sunk soon after. Later, however, the U-boats would score two important successes. The aircraft carrier HMS *Ark Royal* and the battleship HMS *Barham* were sunk within a few days of each other, the latter with heavy loss of life.

However, Hitler's diversion of twelve U-boats from the Atlantic effectively gave Allied shipping almost a two-month 'holiday' there at a time when the merchant ships and their escorts badly needed the break. As 1941 drew to an end, Britain was stocked up with supplies and in a stronger psychological position to continue waging the Battle of the Atlantic.

In 1942 Hitler would once again intervene directly in U-boat warfare, insisting on the deployment of more submarines in Norwegian waters. Against most of the evidence he was convinced Churchill was planning to make an attack on Norway. These submarines at least saw action against those convoys going to Russia. They also proved useful as scouts and scavengers when surface raiders were employed against the merchantmen.

After the Battle of the Bismarck Sea, Hitler's rage at the failure of his surface ships resulted in the loss of Admiral Erich Raeder as commander in chief of the German Navy. Raeder was succeeded by Admiral Donitz in January 1943. Donitz would retain his responsibility for U-boats, correctly believing that nobody else had the same knowledge and experience of U-boat warfare as he did.

U-boat headquarters were moved to Berlin, and integrated into the German Admiralty. Things would not be the same, even though Donitz's long-standing chief of staff, Rear Admiral Godt, succeeded him as Flag Officer, U-boats, and Godt's former position was filled by Gunther Hessler, Donitz's son-in-law, and himself a U-boat ace.

Donitz could no longer influence detailed events nor direct the actual battles as he had done in the past. He also had many other

naval preoccupations besides U-boats. In fact, he was to find himself at variance with Hitler, defending the very surface-ship policies over which his predecessor Raeder had lost his job.

Tactics, merging with strategy, also greatly influenced the Battle of the Atlantic. In 1943, tactics altered considerably as new forces were brought to bear. These included the introduction of small aircraft carriers into convoy escort duty, and a determined campaign by Coastal Command to sink the U-boats as they travelled through the Bay of Biscay.

The escort carriers were ships that weighed not much than 10,000 tons and could be built in less than a year. They would account for twenty-six U-boats. While Coastal Command waited to get aircraft that could cover the air 'gap' over the Atlantic, it waged a determined war in the Bay of Biscay. This was almost a private battle between the huge Sunderland flying boats, the Catalinas and Liberators provided by the U.S. and the U-boats. The battle is excellently described in *Conflict Over The Bay*, by Norman Franks (William Kimber, 1986).

Another of its aspects can be studied in Kenneth Poolman's *Focke-Wulf Condor – Scourge* of the Atlantic (MacDonald & Jane's, 1978).

Other tactics are also worthy of separate study in book-length histories. These include the use of 'wolf-packs' of U-boats working together in ocean-wide ambushes, and the countermeasures of the Allied 'hunter-killer' Escort Groups. These special groups, trained to work together, operated directly against the U-boats. They would pursue and and trap them in complex depth charge attacks, leaving the smaller warships of the close escort to stay and protect the merchant ships.

Another factor worth considering is that of morale, in this case that of the U-boat crews. These men were extremely well trained. Even towards the end, when fresh crews were desperately needed, cutbacks in the length and intensity of their training were seldom allowed. If they were not strictly volunteers in the most democratic meaning of the word, they did feel themselves to be a chosen breed. They enjoyed privileges in terms of leave and

Left: the crew of the 4,793-ton German blockade runner *Silvaplane* are about to be taken aboard HMS *Adventure*, under Captain Bowes Lyon. Intercepted by the British warship 200 miles off Brest, the *Silvaplane* was scuttled and blown up by her crew, all of whom were rescued.

Despite the successes of aircraft in attacking U-boats, the main weapon in the Battle of the Atlantic was always the depth charge. Depth charges are ready to be dropped over the stern of a corvette (right), whilst an RAF Coastal Command aircraft arrives to escort the convoy into a British port.

It cannot be repeated often enough that the object of all convoy work (left) in the Battle of the Atlantic was 'the safe and timely arrival' of the merchant ships. Sinking U-boats was an incidental bonus, and each success facilitiated future passages, but it was getting the ships through that really mattered.

It was always important to the morale of merchant seamen in the Battle of the Atlantic to know they had a good chance of being rescued. This picture of survivors from the torpedoed British freighter *Blairlogie*, sitting in a ship's lifeboat aboard a still-neutral U.S. merchantman, the *American Shipper* (right), is clearly posed, but the overall impression is reassuring.

shore comforts not bestowed on many others in the German forces.

This was perhaps deservedly so, for the crews faced real danger and the likelihood of a terrible fate, crushed and suffocated at the bottom of the sea. There was seldom hope of escape – over half the U-boats sunk left no survivors. Where there were survivors they usually numbered only a handful from each submarine, out of a crew of between forty and fifty.

In 1940, there were no survivors at all from eleven of the twenty-three U-boats sunk. In 1941 there were no survivors from fifteen out of thirty-five; and in 1942, fifty-nine of the eighty-five U-boats that went down did so without a single man escaping. In 1943, the year in which the Battle of the Atlantic was finally won, 154 U-boats out of the 238 sunk had no survivors. At the time, most U-boat crews were probably not wholly aware of the odds against them. Whereas they might hear of the loss of an individual boat, full details were seldom announced publicly. Where possible the extent

of such losses were also kept from the submariners.

Another instance where morale was decisive was among merchant seamen, who were so often passive targets. Professional seamen have always had to contend with the perils of the deep and the possibility of death, but not so the younger, wartime-only recruits. Faced with the thought of death by drowning or, more likely, from exposure, they showed considerable courage. Though inevitably there were instances of panic, fear and selfishness when a ship was torpedoed.

A boost for the morale of the merchant seamen came with the advent of rescue ships, merchantmen specially equipped to pick up survivors. Sailing in the 'tail-end charlie' position of a convoy, these would drop back when ships were hit and take the survivors aboard, despite the risk of becoming victims themselves. When no rescue ships were available, or if they had been sunk, the convoy commodore would invite the last ship in each column to take over

The men (right) rescued after eighty-three days in the Atlantic on a raft (left) were a U.S. gunner and two Dutch seamen. Two other crewmen, who were on the raft with them after the ship sank, died during this ordeal. The men lived on rainwater, and such fish as they could catch. They drifted 1,000 miles before being picked up.

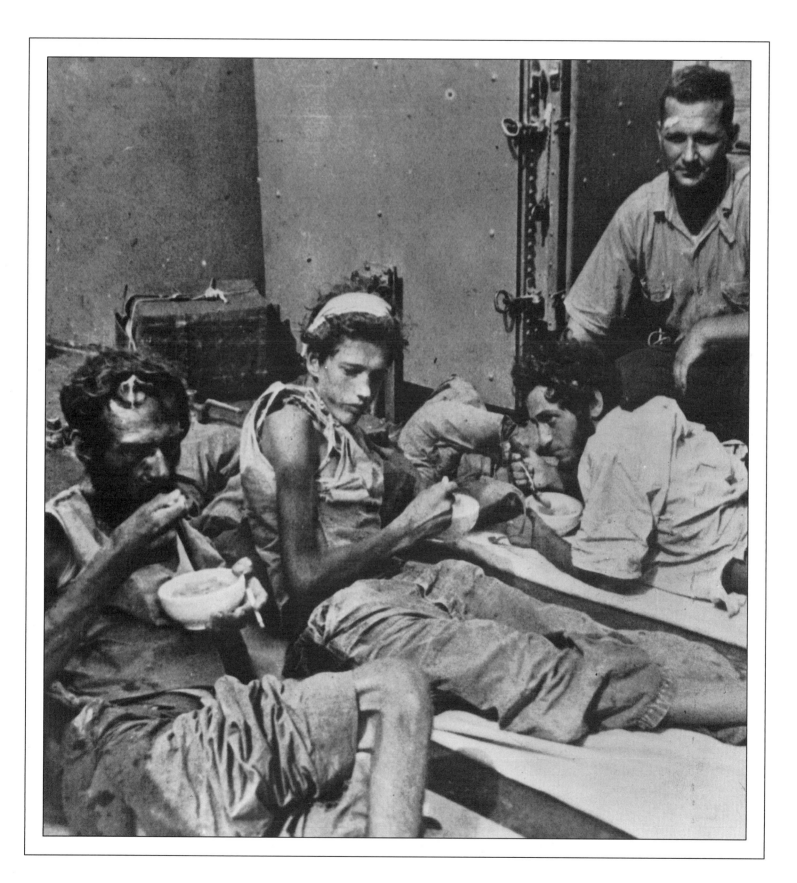

this function. Some coped admirably, despite the extra risk; others declined the invitation and steamed on.

Escort commanders were not supposed to detach warships for rescue work. The escorts were too badly needed to be put at risk by stopping to pick up survivors. Many escort commanders broke these rules, arguing that, if crews were simply abandoned, the morale of the merchant seamen would suffer. They had to be made to feel that they stood at least a fighting chance of survival if they were sunk.

There was no easy solution to this problem. Nor was there any relief from the even more distressing thought that 'total war' could mean machine-gunning survivors in the water. In World War I, Admiral Fisher had said 'the essence of war is violence, and moderation in war is imbecility'. This view would seem to suggest that it would be reasonable for U-boats to kill survivors rather than to let them reach safety and sail again. Similarly, the RAF could stop

dropping life rafts to U-boat men struggling in the waters of the Bay of Biscay.

Luckily, few of those in the Battle of the Atlantic subscribed to Admiral Fisher's opinion. There were reports of boats overturned by submarines travelling fast on the surface that had not seen them. Equally there were times when U-boats were shelled after surfacing to surrender. However, on the whole all seamen were felt to deserve a chance of rescue.

It was, nonetheless, a ruthless, bitter battle, one that was often fought in those appalling weather conditions that have been stressed again and again. Many of those involved had seen their fellows killed, or lost loved ones in enemy bombing raids at home. Generally, however, those thrown into the treacherous waters were regarded not as friend or foe, but merely as 'survivors' who were to be rescued or helped towards safety whenever possible. There is a camaraderie of the sea which transcends even wartime conditions.

Left: the 10,000-ton British motor vessel _Dunbar Castle_ hit a mine on 9 January, 1940 - a reminder that U-boats, surface raiders and German long-range Condor aircraft were not the only hazards faced by ships crossing the Atlantic.

Right: eight identical ships being built at shipyards in Los Angeles. The place where the Battle of the Atlantic was really won was in the shipyards of America on both the east and west coasts. Revolutionary assembly-line procedures for building liberty ships and other merchant vessels ensured that ships were being completed quicker than U-boats could sink them.

D-DAY

D-day was Europe's largest combined operation of all time.

The naval side of the Allied landings in Normandy, overall code name Operation Overlord, was named Operation Neptune. It involved seven battleships, two monitors, twenty-three cruisers, three gunboats, 105 destroyers and over 1,000 smaller naval vessels. The naval tasks were many and varied. They included minesweeping and marking channels in advance, offshore bombardment, escorting and landing the troops, and keeping German destroyers, E-boats and U-boats away from the landings, supplies and reinforcements.

Additionally, the naval forces were involved in the 'Mulberry' harbours scheme. This was to establish two offshore ports made up of sunken blockships, caissons and prefabricated piers and jetties, in total nearly two million tons of concrete and steel. One of the Mulberry harbours would be wrecked by bad weather, but the second was in full operation within a month of D-day. From then on it was no longer necessary for the armies to capture a major Channel port, at least until it was expedient to do so.

Top left: an aerial view of the D-day landings on the Normandy beaches, showing assault craft of all kinds landing men, vehicles and supplies. Another aerial view (bottom left), taken from a B-26 Marauder of the U.S. Ninth Air Force on its way to bomb Avranches in France, gives some idea of the vast armada of ships involved in the D-day landings. In many cases the troops had a considerable distance to go from the point at which they were unloaded from LSIs (Landing Ship, Infantry) (top right) to the beaches. Luckily the weathermen were right in their predictions, and the storms and rough weather of the previous day had generally abated when General Eisenhower decided D-day should go ahead.

Bottom right: the infantryman's view of the D-day landings. Although the landing ramp gave shelter from small-arms fire, the run-in to the beach was a worrying and dangerous moment for all concerned.

The initial credit for the success of Operation Neptune, and an overwhelming success it was, must go to the planners. Nothing on this scale had ever been attempted before, and Hitler's 'Atlantic Wall' constituted the most sophisticated set of defences any amphibious landing would ever face. Although the troops manning the coastal defences were not of a universally high calibre, the Germans still had considerable *Panzer* forces in France. Luckily, owing to doubts about where the Allies would land, most of these armoured units were a long way from Normandy from the outset.

One problem that hit the planners rather at the last minute was the need for extra ships. General Eisenhower and his deputy, General Montgomery, decided at a late stage that the assault must be on a five-division front and not, as originally planned, on a three-division front. With only weeks to go, the planners had to borrow extra forces from the Atlantic convoys, the Home Fleet and the Mediterranean, and to divert ships destined for the Far East and the Pacific.

The second problem was predicting the weather, and trying to choose the best date on which to land. The meteorologists forecast a Channel storm and gale-force winds in the Irish Sea on the chosen date of 5 June. They were proved correct and D-day was postponed for twenty-four hours. Some convoys already at sea had to 'mark time', and one that did not get the recall signal had to be intercepted by aircraft and turned back. The weathermen

predicted better conditions for 6 June, and for at least another day thereafter. General Eisenhower took the decision to go.

The pattern of the landings has been exhaustively described in hundreds of military books. All that is needed here is to stress what a truly giant combined operation of all three services it was. 5, a hundred heavy and medium bombers and 5,400 fighter aircraft provided the air support. 2,300 transports ferried the three airborne divisions, the 82nd and 101st U.S. Airborne and the British 6th Airborne to their landing grounds in Normandy.

The naval contribution began during the night. About a hundred minesweepers went in from both the Western and Eastern Naval Task Forces, to clear the route of mines and to drop marker buoys. The crews of midget submarines who had an extra twenty-four-hour wait off Normandy because of the postponement, signalled the routes ashore, and frogmen dealt with some of the beach defences.

Then the naval bombardment commenced. This was not as effective as had been hoped, and many big German guns and defensive positions survived the shells. Nevertheless it was heartening for Allied morale and, coupled with the air domination, disheartening for the enemy.

At the far western, or American, end of the forty-mile front, the U.S. battleship *Nevada* and the British monitor HMS *Erebus* provided the big guns. A mixed Allied force of five cruisers and ten destroyers provided the necessary closer supporting fire for 'Utah' beach, where the 4th

U.S. Infantry Division were first ashore. Two more U.S. battleships, the *Texas* and the *Arkansas*, three cruisers and another ten destroyers shelled 'Omaha' beach, where the 1st U.S. Infantry Division was the first to land. In support, as an offshore reserve for the Western Task Force, was the battleship HMS *Nelson* along with more cruisers and destroyers.

Much the same pattern of support was repeated on the three eastern beaches. These were 'Gold', near Arromanches (British 50th Division), 'Juno', near Courcelles (3rd Canadian Infantry Division) and 'Sword', near Lyon-sur-Mer (British 3rd Division). At 'Gold' there were four British cruisers, a Dutch gunboat and thirteen destroyers. At 'Juno' there were two cruisers and a very mixed Allied force of eleven destroyers. At the far end, 'Sword', drew the fire of two of the older British battleships, HMS *Warspite* and HMS *Ramillies*, along with a monitor, five cruisers and yet another thirteen destroyers. There was also another offshore reserve for the Eastern Task Force, including the

battleship HMS *Rodney*.

The preliminary bombardment was followed by much close support work, mainly provided by the cruisers and destroyers. Then it was time for the landings to begin. Preceded by rocket assault craft, mostly manned by the Royal Marines, the great armada of landing craft headed for their designated beaches. 20,000 5-inch rockets were fired on the three eastern beaches, and about 18,000 on the two western ones. In all, some 4,000 landing craft of every size, shape and function were employed on Operation Neptune.

The planners must again be commended here. Incorporated into the D-day landings was almost every lesson that had been learned since Operation Torch, eighteen months earlier, and since the landings in Sicily and Italy in 1943. One of the most important of these lessons was the value of efficient communications between those doing the fighting and those directing from offshore. The five headquarters ships: the *Bayfield* ('Utah'), the *Ancon*

Left: a reminder of the cost of war - one soldier who did not get across the beach. The picture also shows some of the beach defences designed to wreck landing craft as they came in on a higher tide.

Top right: an aerial view of a Mulberry Harbour off the Normandy beaches. Two artificial ports, each as big as the British colony of Gibraltar, were built in Britain and towed across the Channel. These allowed heavy equipment and supplies to be landed, an operation that would only otherwise have been possible by capturing a French port.

Bottom right: army jeeps driving through a gentle surf for the last hundred yards after debouching from their LCV's (Landing Craft, Vehicles)

Bottom far right: 'Omaha' Beach, Normandy, with a floating dock jetty over which reinforcements could arrive dry shod. Offshore a line of protective blockships, purposely sunk, act as a breakwater.

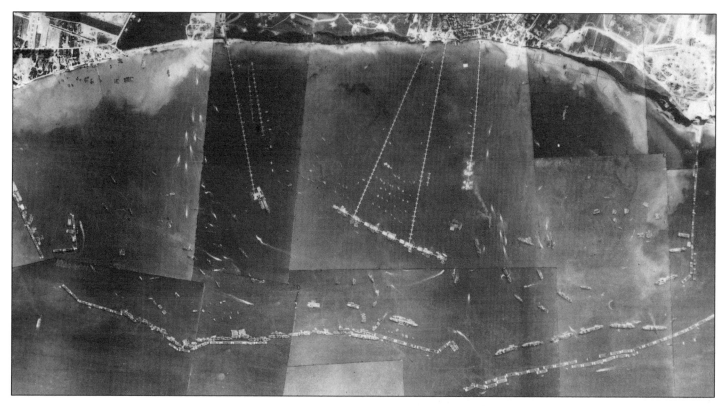

('Omaha'), the *Bulolo* ('Gold'), the *Hilary* ('Juno') and the *Largs* ('Sword') proved their worth time and time again.

Sixteen hours after the D-day landings began, over 132,000 men were ashore: 23,250 at 'Utah', 34,250 at 'Omaha', 24,970 at 'Gold', 21,400 at 'Juno' and 28,845 at 'Sword'. Of course, none of this was achieved without loss. The American landings at 'Omaha' got off to a particularly bad start. There were delays in getting ashore and confusion as craft arrived at the wrong landing place and in the wrong order. 'Bunching' occurred as successive waves of craft arrived to find their predecessors held up by withering German fire.

Generally speaking, naval losses were small. German air attacks sank two destroyers, USS *Meredith II* and HMS *Boniface*. Three U.S. and three British destroyers were lost after striking mines, and a French destroyer was sunk by coastal artillery. A number of transports and

other smaller naval vessels also struck mines.

Needless to say there were steady losses among the landing ships and assault craft, throughout Operation Neptune. British losses included the Landing Ship, Infantry (Large), the *Empire Broadsword*, and the Landing Ship, Infantry (Small), the *Prince Leopold*. The former was mined off Normandy, the latter torpedoed by a U-boat in the English Channel.

184 Landing Craft, Assault were lost, plus four of the Hedgerow rocket ships. Thirty-six Landing Craft, Mechanised (Mark I) were sunk, as were forty-two of the heavier, fifty-two-ton Landing Craft, Mechanised (Mark III). There were losses among all sizes of Landing Craft, Personnel and Landing Craft, Vehicle and among the whole range of specialist support craft, from oiler barges to water carriers.

Unlike in the Pacific, where almost every amphibious operation was threatened by a possible Japanese naval strike force, Operation

Neptune faced no such danger from surface attack.

By June 1944, all Hitler's capital ships and heavy cruisers had been accounted for. The mighty *Tirpitz*, seriously damaged by British midget submarines in Trondheim, had been put out of action again, thisn time in a thorough Fleet Air Arm raid on 3 April, 1944. The last operational German battleship, the *Scharnhorst* had been sunk by HMS *Duke of York* in the Battle of North Cape on 26 December, 1943. This was probably the last direct fight between battleships to take place, and it marked the end of Germany as a naval power.

All that was left, therefore, to oppose the D-day landings was a handful of destroyers, torpedo boats and E-boats based at Le Havre and Brest, and the U-boat fleets from the Bay of Biscay. One sally from Le Havre against the Eastern Task Force saw the sinking of the Norwegian destroyer the *Svenner*. The two British battleships and the headquarters ship off 'Sword' beach, were also narrowly missed by torpedoes. A destroyer raid from Brest was intercepted, resulting in the sinking of one German destroyer and the beaching of another, which was then blown up.

Otherwise the majority of the fighting was between Allied MTBs and German E-boats.

Though this was spirited and often vicious, it never represented a major threat to either the landings or the supplies. A good deal of mining was carried out, causing losses to both sides as did the gunfire.

The U-boats posed a much greater potential threat, but the Neptune planners had deployed considerable forces to meet this. No.19 Group RAF Coastal Command had been heavily reinforced for this purpose. Almost all the Atlantic support groups, the 'hunter-killer' destroyers, sloops and frigate escorts, had been withdrawn from convoy work and concentrated in the Western Approaches.

Four to six groups operated in the area west of the Channel and in the Bay of Biscay, two others protected the entrance to the Channel itself. Three escort carriers were there to provide support.

As soon as it was known that the D-day landings were taking place, the U-boats set out: seventeen from Brest, fourteen from St.Nazaire, four from La Pallice, and one from Lorient. However, aircraft were waiting for them. Two homeward-bound U-boats were sunk, and four of the U-boats from Brest were damaged and had to return. Three more U-boats were sunk over the next two days.

It was clear that any U-boat without a snorkel would not be able to enter the English Channel,

Left: the breakwaters formed by deliberately sunken freighters helped to break up the waves during a storm shortly after D-day. In all, twenty-three ships were sunk to make this particular sea defence.

Right: wounded
soldiers being
evacuated from
Normandy aboard
a U.S. Coast Guard
LCT (Landing Craft,
Tank)

A royal visitor to Normandy. General Eisenhower's deputy, General Bernard Montgomery, explaining the war situation to King George VI at his headquarters in France.

and only nine of them were thus equipped, though other snorkel boats came down from Norway. The U-boats that tried to enter the D-day operational area were soon engaged in fierce battles with destroyers.

By 14 June, some U-boats had penetrated the landing areas, to find that the support groups were there too. The U-boats scored some successes, accounting for Landing Ship, Tank 280, the frigate *Mourne* and the destroyer escort HMS *Blackwood*.

However, the U-boats were also going down. U-767 and U-441 went down on 14 June, followed by U-971, U-1191 and U-269 over the next few days. U-988 also sank, but not before fatally torpedoeing the corvette HMS *Pink*.

The U-boat battle raged on for several days. Two snorkel U-boats carried out some mining off Plymouth and Lands End, and claimed at least one transport victim.

The statistics, however, show how forlorn these attempts to interfere with the landings were. What mattered was not the number of ships sunk, nor even how many U-boats were depth-charged into oblivion, but the number of the ships that arrived safely and on time.

By the end of June, a total of 570 Liberty ships, 788 coastal boats, 905 LSTs, 1442 LCTs, 180 troop transports and 371 LCIs had reached France safely in supply convoys. 130,000 troops landed on D-day itself; six days later 326,000 troops, 54,000 vehicles and 100,000 tons of supplies were ashore. By 2 July, the Allied forces in France consisted of four corps of the United States 1st Army and four Corps of the 2nd British Army. They numbered very nearly one million men, and were equipped with 177,000 vehicles and half a million tons of supplies.

There was still another year of fighting ahead, but after the success of Operation Overlord, with the naval contribution of Operation Neptune, the question of which side would win in the end was never again in real doubt. Ultimate victory was now just a matter of time.

BATTLES OFF GUADALCANAL

Midway marked the first major check to Japanese aggression and expansion since their attack on Pearl Harbor. It was a significant American victory. However, wars are only won on the ground. Lost territory must be recovered and, ultimately, the enemy's capital must be occupied.

More than three years' hard fighting, on land and against a determined enemy, lay ahead of the United States. Although her Australian and New Zealand allies were also sometimes fully involved, the Pacific island battlegrounds were mainly American. Land battles would not concern us here, were it not for the fact that 'island hopping', as it came to be called, inevitably meant the use of amphibious forces.

The U.S. Marines, and the U.S. Army divisions that followed them, had to be escorted to their landing places offshore. They required as much support and protection as possible, and they had to be continually supplied and reinforced as they fought their way towards Tokyo. The warships also had to stop enemy supplies and reinforcements getting through.

The first U.S. objective was Guadalcanal, one of the British Solomon Islands on the northern edge of the Coral Sea. The assault, originally planned for later in 1942, was brought forward to August. This was because the Japanese, who already had a seaplane base on nearby Tulagi, were discovered to be building an airfield in the jungle in the north of Guadalcanal. This would become Henderson Field, a key to the six-month battle for the island which followed.

The amphibious forces for the landing were under the command of Vice Admiral Robert Ghormley U.S.N. Task Force 62, under Rear Admiral Turner, had nineteen transports, carrying 19,000 U.S. Marines. It was escorted by three 8-inch gun cruisers, one 6-inch gun cruiser, and eight destroyers. This escort force included

Australian ships, and was commanded by British Rear Admiral Victor Crutchley R.N., who had won a Victoria Cross in World War I. There were also four more cruisers and six more destroyers making up two fire support groups.

Operating to the south was the powerful Task Force 61, under the command of Rear Admiral Fletcher. Along with the three aircraft carriers, the *Saratoga*, the *Enterprise* and the *Wasp*, this force also boasted a fast new battleship, the USS *North Carolina* and six 8-inch gun cruisers.

Opposing them was the much smaller Japanese Eighth Fleet, based to the north at Rabaul in New Britain. It was commanded by Vice Admiral Gunichi Mikawa, second in command of the attack on Pearl Harbor, and also at Midway. His force included five 8-inch gun cruisers, two smaller cruisers and destroyers. Added to this were naval aircraft operating from land: twenty-four bombers and thirty fighters.

At this stage the main Japanese fleet was far away, though heavy reinforcements would arrive for later battles off Guadalcanal. For Guadalcanal was a whole series of naval battles, not all of which the Americans won. At least two were disastrous in terms of losses. In his

excellent book, *Naval Battles of World War II*, Captain Geoffrey Bennett R.N points out that the U.S.A. fought as many sea battles around Guadalcanal as the Royal Navy had fought in the whole of World War I.

D-day at Guadalcanal and Tulagi was 7 August, 1942. The fact that the date had been advanced meant that the U.S. Marines were only able to stage one practice landing at Fiji. Nor had the supporting force, of mixed Australian and American cruisers, had the chance of working together before going into action.

In fact, the landings went surprisingly well. By the following afternoon, after fierce fighting, 6,000 marines had captured Tulagi. 11,000 marines landed on Guadalcanal with virtually only one Japanese labour battalion engaged on building the airfield to resist them. However, there were still more men to land and supplies to get ashore. The naval fire support groups and Rear Admiral Crutchley's cruiser force were then reorganised to cover any Japanese naval intrusions from either east or west.

The chapter of accidents that followed was blamed by some on the British admiral's dispositions. Either out of tact, or in the cause of Allied solidarity, he was not criticised by the

An apparently peaceful Pacific island (left), where the Guadalcanal waterway meets the Pacific, was actually the site of the battle of Matinakau. Wrecked Japanese tanks can be seen in the Matanikau River.

U.S. Marines are seen soon after landing with their jeeps (right) from what was, in 1942, a new type of landing barge. Jeeps came into their own as ideal vehicles for the kind of fighting that took place on Guadalcanal and other Pacific islands.

American commander in chief, Admiral King, in a later summing-up of the battle.

Instead of deploying his force well out to the west, with a destroyer screen even further out, Rear Admiral Crutchley chose to stay east of Savo Island, situated just to the north of Guadalcanal. He also managed to be away attending a conference with the Americans, when the Japanese arrived. He had travelled to the conference on his flagship, HMAS *Australia* instead of using one of the destroyers, thus splitting the defending forces even more.

The conference had been called after Rear Admiral Fletcher, commanding the aircraft carriers, gave notice that he was withdrawing his force that night and would not provide air cover for the third day's landings. Rear Admiral Turner, in charge of the landings, protested, but Fletcher was senior to him. Remembering his loss of the *Yorktown* at Midway, Fletcher stuck by his decision. A month or so later, Fletcher would be relieved of his command of aircraft carriers, and 'promoted' to take charge in the

Top left: the liner *Kinugawa Maru*, a Japanese casualty at Guadalcanal. After failing to defeat the U.S. Navy in a series of battles off Guadalcanal, the Japanese were reduced to running fast night-time 'Tokyo Express' convoys in an attempt to land reinforcements on the islands the Americans were attacking.

Bottom left: the U.S. aircraft carrier *Wasp*, one of the two American carriers to be lost during the series of naval battles off Guadalcanal.

Right: three Americans lie dead on a beach at Buna in New Guinea. U.S. policy about showing the bodies of Americans killed in action in the official pictures of battle scenes changed in early 1943. It was felt that the public should be made to understand the real cost of war and the sacrifices involved.

Left: Australian troops about to land from American landing craft at Sadau, an island six miles north of Tarakan, Borneo. As island hopping continued through the latter part of the war in the Pacific, the Australians became involved in action in many places.

remote backwaters of the North Pacific Area.

The Japanese did exactly what they might have been expected to do – they headed straight for Guadalcanal and the vulnerable transports. Led by the large 8-inch gun cruiser *Chokai*, their force was now about the same size as that guarding the western approaches, given that HMAS *Australia* was absent and other cruisers had been detached to guard the east. The forces might have been equal in gun power, but the Japanese were three times as powerful in terms of torpedoes. A total of forty-eight Japanese torpedo tubes were able to use the Japanese Long Lance 24-inch torpedo.

The Japanese were sighted early on by a U.S. submarine, which had to dive under the passing ships, being too close to fire her torpedoes. In the darkness the submarine underestimated the enemy's strength in her subsequent radio report. The Japanese then steamed right past the two patrolling picket destroyers that Crutchley had placed. Nobody had thought of coordinating their sweeps. Thus when they were each at the end of their patrol there was a gap left in the middle. Vice Admiral Mikawa's force passed straight through this, undetected by either picket's radar or lookouts.

Most of the details of the one-sided battle that followed are best forgotten. Suffice to recall that half the crews on the Allied cruisers were asleep and that their guns were all trained fore-and-aft. The Japanese launched their attack unseen, and HMAS *Canberra* was hit immediately by two torpedoes as well as by broadsides from Japanese guns. The USS *Chicago* was hit by another torpedo.

The U.S. cruiser fired star shell but none of it ignited. Eventually the *Chicago* steamed off in pursuit, but Mikawa's ships had split and no contact was made. The *Chicago's* next move, on what was admittedly an extremely dark night, was to return and fire shells at the destroyer USS *Patterson*, standing by the stricken *Canberra*. Luckily none of the shells scored a hit.

The Japanese continued to wreak havoc, smashing three U.S. cruisers, the *Astoria*, the *Quincy* and the *Vincennes*, with broadsides, scoring hits with torpedoes, and setting all three ablaze. Two sank, and the *Astoria* survived only as a burning hulk. There was a total loss of 900 lives.

Despite this catalogue of disasters, the Allied naval forces fulfilled their primary objective of protecting the transports. They did so only because Vice Admiral Mikawa lost control of his divided force, and had to sail north to regroup them. There, fearing that next day he would be attacked by planes from the American aircraft carriers that he thought were still in the area, he decided to head back to Rabaul, the main Japanese base.

On the way, the U.S. submarine S-44 managed to torpedo and sink the cruiser *Kato*, the only outright Japanese loss in this battle.

This unhappy first battle off Guadalcanal – the Battle of Savo Island – illustrates so many of the overall problems of battle at sea. There were the usual communication and reporting difficulties, there were problems of command and tactics, but above all there was a failure to appreciate the enemy's potential.

In fighting a truly determined and professional force, which is what the Japanese Navy proved, the Allied cruisers had failed to measure up and it had cost them dearly. However, it was a good introduction to what they would be up against, both on Guadalcanal and on other Pacific islands.

Several of the subsequent battles at sea off Guadalcanal concerned the so-called Tokyo Express convoys of destroyers and transports taking reinforcements to the island. These fast-moving convoys were protected by their own aircraft carriers and battleships, and challenged by those of the Americans.

A little over two weeks after the Battle of Savo Island, the Americans sank the small carrier *Ryujo*, but suffered serious damage to the USS *Enterprise*. A week later, a Japanese submarine torpedoed the USS *Yorktown*, putting her in dock for three months. On 15 September, 1942, another Japanese submarine attacked a force covering some American transports. It sank the U.S. aircraft carrier *Wasp* and a destroyer, and also damaged the battleship *North Dakota*.

The next battle, Cape Esperance, was a clear U.S. victory, except in its failure to stop the Tokyo Express reinforcements getting through. In this conflict the American force sank an 8-inch gun cruiser and a destroyer, badly damaged another Japanese cruiser, and killed Rear Admiral Goto of Coral Sea fame.

On 22 October, the Japanese Fleet was present in strength as their land forces made a fierce attempt to capture Henderson Field. Three powerful Japanese naval forces, including four carriers, steamed southwards to intercept Task Force 64, under Vice Admiral Lee. Taskforce 64 consisted of a battleship and three cruisers. Unbeknownst to the Japanese, two other American task forces, each including an aircraft carrier, were also preparing to engage.

When they did eventually locate all these forces, more than 130 Japanese aircraft flew off from the four carriers to attack. The USS *Hornet* was seriously damaged, and later sank, the USS *Enterprise* only slightly so. In return, U.S. aircraft caused extensive damage to two Japanese carriers, the *Zuiho* and the *Shokaku*, putting the latter out of action for six months. In addition the Japanese lost many more aircraft than the Americans.

This battle was seen as a tactical victory for the Japanese, but one which they failed to exploit fully. They missed a golden opportunity to pursue and sink the *Enterprise*. Furthermore, they did not capture Henderson Field, which the Marines tenaciously managed to maintain.

The next battle, the Battle of Guadalcanal, came in November. In the first stage, a force of American cruisers and destroyers bravely intercepted a stronger Japanese force that included two capital ships, the *Hiyei* and the *Kirishima*.

In the night action that followed the Americans would lose two cruisers, the *Atlanta* and the *Juneau*, and four destroyers. The Japanese lost just two destroyers, but the *Hiyei* was so badly damaged she had to retire. She would be torpedoed next day by aircraft from the USS *Enterprise*, bombed by shore-based aircraft, then eventually abandoned and scuttled.

These losses more or less balanced out to make battle honours even. However, the Japanese had again been stopped from getting at the American transports that were continuing to land men and supplies on Guadalcanal.

Next day, 14 November, 1942, other Japanese forces bombarded Henderson Field, destroying or damaging fifty aircraft. Nevertheless, the airfield could still be used and torpedo planes from it seriously damaged two Japanese cruisers, one of which, the *Kinugasa*, was later sunk by torpedo bombers from the *Enterprise*.

The final stage of this series of battles within a battle saw aircraft, from both Henderson

Burning oil tanks ashore on Sadau, as the Australian force heads inwards. The following day there were landings on Tarakan itself.

Field and the *Enterprise*, attacking Japanese troop transports heading towards the airfield. These ships were supported by a large bombardment force consisting of the remaining Japanese battleship, the *Kirishima;* four cruisers and eight destroyers.

Heading to intercept them was a force, under Vice Admiral Lee, of two battleships and four destroyers. These battleships, the *Washington* and the *South Dakota*, were brand-new sister ships, heavily armoured and equipped with radar. The Japanese did not yet have radar.

Another confused night action followed, in which the Americans were hindered by the malfunction of the *South Dakota's* radar. The *South Dakota* was lucky to escape more than thirty torpedoes fired at her. However, she was hit by 14-inch shells from the Japanese battleship and 8-inch ones from two cruisers. She pulled out of the battle with a hundred casualties, and had to go back to the U.S.A for repairs. The radar on the *Washington* worked well. She shattered the *Kirishima*, which was later scuttled.

The real American triumph came when Admiral Kondo decided to withdraw and not to bombard Henderson Field after all. When the Japanese transports arrived at dawn and prepared to land their troops, they were fiercely attacked by planes from the still functioning Henderson Field. Only about 2,000 out of the intended 11,000 reinforcements finally reached Guadalcanal.

Fighting in the seas off Guadalcanal continued for another two months, although the Japanese were now restricted to making quick Tokyo Express supply trips and did not try any further major landings.

Cataloguing the losses on either side at Guadalcanal depends on where you start counting. In general the Americans would seem to have won a slight edge. Overall they lost two aircraft carriers, nine cruisers, eighteen destroyers, and several transports and auxiliaries. The Japanese lost two carriers, although one was fairly small, two battleships, eight cruisers and thirty-eight destroyers.

In January, the Japanese decided to abandon Guadalcanal. By February they had all slipped quietly away. The first link in the island chain had been forged.

BATTLE OF THE PHILIPPINE SEA

In August 1944, President Roosevelt met his two Pacific commanders in chief, General Douglas MacArthur and Admiral Chester W. Nimitz, aboard a U.S. cruiser in Pearl Harbo, to discuss the next steps in the war in the Pacific.

One of the biggest developments in warfare at sea during the Second World War was this use of amphibious forces for island hopping.

World War I had been almost entirely a matter of giant armies fighting it out on land. Apart from the original Battle of the Atlantic and one major naval engagement, Jutland, all the conclusive fighting between 1914 and 1918 took place on the continent of Europe.

By the Second World War the situation had completely changed. The Allies had to fight their way back onto that very continent. They also had to defeat the Japanese in fighting for hundreds of islands scattered across the whole length and breadth of the Pacific Ocean.

In the course of doing so, they had to develop a new dimension of sea warfare: the amphibious assault. This required almost a new science of warfare, with skills and techniques all of its own.

The Japanese, in their successful sweep through the southwest Pacific, never needed to develop such techniques. Instead, they specialised in landing small parties from destroyers and cruisers. These parties would then make their way through generally undefended jungle and attack where least expected. The Germans, however, were never to launch Operation 'Sealion', their planned cross-Channel invasion of Britain, and their attack on Crete relied heavily on parachute troops and command of the air. Amphibious

Lofoten Islands and Vaagso in 1941, and in the attack on Dieppe in 1942. The North African landings of Operation Torch, though this was anything but a copybook exercise, gave the Allies further experience, as did the landings in Sicily and Italy.

However, it would be in the Pacific, from 1942, that the real art of amphibious warfare would be developed. After Guadalcanal, there were American assaults in support of the Australians fighting in New Guinea. The Americans would progress up the Solomons, into the Bismarck Archipelago and New Britain, and thence on to Guam, the Philippines, Iwo Jima and Okinawa.

Hindsight enables historians to discern patterns and make judgements that are not always so obvious at the time. Most historians appear to agree that the U.S. seemed almost to be fighting two separate campaigns in the

warfare needed new types of vessel, new types of forces.

Once again, it was American production methods that held the key to success. Over three years, the U.S.A. produced 45,000 vessels of varying design, and 56,000 amphibious vehicles. The Allies found new specialists to man the landing craft and to build and maintain the beachheads that had to serve as ports.

The British used mainly Royal Marines and "hostilities only" sailors from the Royal Naval Volunteer Reserve for their landing craft. The Americans relied on the U.S. Marines, who were traditionally responsible for amphibious operations. Added to these, however, were many Navy men, Coast Guards, and Army engineers, to create a fully integrated force.

The British had had some limited experience in amphibious assault both raiding against the

A Japanese aircraft is hit on 10 October, 1944. It was later sunk. As the War moved northwards towards Japan, carrier-borne aircraft from Admiral Halsey's Third Fleet began removing the remnants of Japanese shipping from the Pacific.

Pacific: the Army game and the Navy game. Each campaign involved amphibious warfare and inter-service cooperation, but the overall strategies were not always as well coordinated as they should have been. Whether this resulted from the absence of one overall supreme commander or from the singularly strong personality of General MacArthur will probably never be satisfactorily resolved.

In his drive from the southwest into the central Pacific, MacArthur appeared to see things differently from those planning the Navy game to the north. There were occasions when his promise to the Philippines: 'I will return', seemed to take precedence over the main strategy of defeating Japan and occupying Tokyo.

It seems cruel perhaps to leapfrog quickly over the thirty months of bitter fighting that took place between the battles of Guadalcanal and Iwo Jima. The names of the islands that saw action during this period will

for ever be imprinted upon the American consciousness, but, American success in mastering the practice of amphibious warfare meant that, after Guadalcanal, nobody doubted that each successive landing would succeed. These landings included Tarawa in the Gilbert Islands in 1943, Eniwetok in the Marshalls and Saipan in the Marianas in 1944, the Philippines from October 1944 onwards, and then Iwo Jima and Okinawa in 1945.

From the navy's point of view, its involvement did not differ greatly from island to island. The U.S. Task Forces had to prevent the Japanese interfering with the troop landings, and ensure the safe arrival of supplies and reinforcements. They carried out preliminary bombardments, and were often involved later in providing close supporting fire. They also had to intercept any attempt by the Japanese to send reinforcements to their own island garrisons and, where possible, prevent supplies getting through.

Top left: an aerial view of Iwo Jima gives an idea of the minute size of the island, despite which it saw some of the fiercest fighting of the Pacific war. The American invasion armada can be seen offshore.

Bottom left: rockets from a U.S. rocket ship hurtle towards the Japanese defences. Okinawa suffered some of the fiercest pre-invasion bombardment of any island during the Pacific war.

Right: 16-inch shells from a U.S. battleship can be clearly seen in the top left-hand corner of the picture as they are fired towards Okinawa.

Vice Admiral Marc A. Mitchner (left), one of the first officers in the U.S. Navy to receive a pilot's certificate, made his name as a commander of aircraft carrier forces in the Pacific. In 1944 he took command of the First Carrier Task Force which was to become famous as Task Force 58.

Right: Admiral William F. Halsey was another naval officer who qualified as an aviator. From early 1942, he was involved in almost every action in the Pacific that included aircraft carriers, and he was in command of the American force that won the Battle of Cape Engano on 25 October, 1944. He later commanded the Third Fleet at Okinawa, and in attacks on Japan itself.

In this latter task the U.S. forces were greatly helped by the way in which their submarines had come to dominate the waters of the Pacific. A good example of this came in the southwest Pacific in April/May 1944. The Japanese were trying to run a convoy of reinforcements to positions in the Halmahera islands of the Dutch East Indies.

A convoy carrying 20,000 Japanese troops left Shanghai in China, travelling through Philippine waters towards Halmahera. On 26 April, 1944 the USS *Jack* sank the transport *Yoshida Maru* off Manila Bay. Ten days later three more ships fell to the USS *Gurnard*. Nearly half that force of 20,000 men never arrived.

What the island battles *did* prove was that the Japanese would not surrender. Most of their garrisons died fighting, and only miniscule numbers were prepared to become prisoners of war. At Kwajelein Atoll, the Americans lost

372 dead and, 1,582 wounded. Of the Japanese garrison of 8,675, only 265 surrendered. Similarly, Eniwetok cost the Americans 195 dead, and 521 wounded but of the 3,431 strong Japanese garrison, only sixty-four surrendered.

Figures such as these made it clear that the more islands that could safely be bypassed the better. They also confirmed that the final invasion of Japan would be just as costly as the planners had feared.

Before passing on to the only significant naval battle before the Battles of the Leyte Gulf, it is perhaps appropriate to pay tribute to those who manned the landing craft in these island landings. Their key contribution should never be dismissed lightly. A good analysis of the craft used and their development during the War is contained in *Assault from the Sea* by J.W. Land. From the merchant seamen aboard

A fleet of U.S. aircraft carriers at sea in 1945.

an LSS (Landing Ship, Stern-chute) to the men who manned an LBK (Landing Barge, Kitchen), we should remember the crews who were the heart of each operation's success, and the men who sailed the first waves of assault craft onto the beach.

British craft were generally manned by a coxswain, a gunner/bowman, and a mechanic/engine-man who would also help with ropes at the rear of the craft. They were at the 'sharp end' of each and every amphibious operation in Europe, and suffered casualties accordingly. They and their American brethren in the Pacific deserve greater attention in books about naval warfare than they have on the whole been accorded to date.

A naval battle that illustrates the new role the submarine played in the Pacific is the Battle of the Philippine Sea, 19/21 June, 1944. To support the Marianas operation some nineteen American submarines were placed in position off Formosa, the Philippines and the Marianas. Another nine submarines from the U.S. Seventh Fleet provided reinforcements.

No sooner had the Japanese begun preparing their fleet for action than the submarines began to take their toll. The USS *Harder* sank the destroyers *Minatsuki*, *Hayanami* and *Tanikaze* off Tawi-Tawi. As the very strong Japanese force moved off, it was reported by one U.S. submarine; then, as the carriers went through the San Bernardino Strait, they were reported by another; and the presence of battleships east of Mindanao was reported by yet another submarine.

These warnings gave Admiral Spruance time to assemble the full body of Task Force 58 west of the Marianas to cover the American landing operations. Spruance faced a main force, under Vice Admiral Takao Kurita, of four Japanese battleships, three carriers, five cruisers and eight destroyers; and two separate carrier forces:

155

Carrier Force 'A', under Vice Admiral Jisaburo Ozawa, had the brand-new *Taiho*, the sturdy faithfuls *Shokaku* and *Zuikaku*; three cruisers and six destroyers; Carrier Force 'B', under Rear Admiral Joshima, had three more aircraft carriers, the *Junyo*, the *Hiyo* and the *Ryuho*, plus a battleship, cruisers and destroyers.

The Japanese located various elements of TF58, and, on the morning of 19th June, 1944, sent off 372 aircraft in four waves. The advance warning given by the submarines and the American advantage of radar, however, allowed their fighters to intercept quickly. Supported by anti-aircraft fire from the U.S. battleships and their escorts, the fighters enjoyed the greatest air victory of the War. It came to be known as 'The Great Marianas Turkey Shoot'.

242 of the Japanese aircraft were shot down. Others were destroyed when they landed on Guam to refuel. Although they scored a hit on the USS *South Dakota*, none of the strikes really threatened the U.S. aircraft carriers.

Meanwhile, the U.S. submarine *Albacore* torpedoed the aircraft carrier *Taiho*, which later exploded and sank, taking three quarters of her crew with her. In her turn the USS *Cavalla* torpedoed and sank the *Shokaku*. Next day, American aircraft caught the Japanese refuelling, and a third carrier, the *Hiyo*, was sunk, together with two tankers. Three further carriers, including the *Zuikaku*, and a battleship were damaged.

Twenty U.S. aircraft were lost. However, despite the carriers turning on their lights, the main American losses came when their planes returned. Seventy-two were lost in crashes on deck or had to crash-land in the sea alongside. Out of 209 crews, 160 survived.

The Japanese withdrew and, though tempted to pursue them with his battleships, Admiral Spruance stayed to fulfil his primary task of protecting the Marianas landings. It was a great American victory, and an indication of things to come in the carrier battles that would follow in the following months.

A giant amphibious force steams towards the Philippines - Transports, LSTs and smaller vessels cover the water.

Four separate battles are generally grouped together under the overall title of Leyte Gulf. These are the battles of the Sibuyan Sea, the Surigao Strait, Samar and Cape Engano.

Each was a very different engagement from the others, and each provides important lessons to be learned. Together they marked a last desperate attempt on the part of the Japanese to halt the now unstoppable American advance on their country. The Leyte battles did not end the war in the Pacific, which continued for almost a year. However, each battle, as a conclusive American victory, indicated the way fortunes were inevitably turning.

Assembled for the battles were the largest fleets either side had ever produced. The D-day armada invading Normandy probably involved slightly larger numbers, but the U.S. Third and Seventh Fleets added together formed the most powerful naval force of all time.

The invasion of the Philippines, originally planned for December 1944, was brought forward to October. The United States 6th Army would land on the eastern side of Leyte, just south of Samar. Air support was to come from land-based U.S.AAF aircraft operating from nearby islands and from the main American carrier force, a part of the U.S. Third Fleet, under Admiral W.F. Halsey. Added to this there were three task forces, consisting of six escort carriers each and forming part of the U.S. Seventh Fleet, under Vice Admiral Kinkaid. Vice Admiral Kinkaid also had a fire support and bombardment force of six battleships, three heavy cruisers, two light cruisers and sixteen destroyers.

The problem of the difference between the navy and the army approach has been mentioned elsewhere and is exemplified here. Vice Admiral Kinkaid took his orders from General MacArthur, whilst Admiral Halsey was directly responsible to Admiral Nimitz. At one stage this nearly spelled disaster. Halsey stuck to what he had been told was his overriding task, to destroy the Japanese carrier force, and

A U.S. battleship, screened by fleet destroyers, steams into position (top left) to begin a bombardment of the Japanese in the Philippines.

A close-up of battleships of the U.S. Seventh Fleet in formation (bottom left) in Lingayen Gulf prior to bombarding Luzon. Some of the ships were amongst those salvaged from Pearl Harbor.

General MacArthur returns to the Philippines. On 20 October, 1944, landings began on Leyte Island (right) and over the following three days a total of 200,000 troups came ashore.

incorrectly assumed that Kinkaid had taken precautions to stop the Japanese coming through the Surigao Strait and getting at the landing force.

However, all that came later. Air attacks and bombardments preceded the landing on 20 October and, as soon as the Japanese were sure where the U.S. attack was aimed, they began moving in their forces in strength from Brunei, in Borneo, and elsewhere. Halsey's Third Fleet was guarding the north, and Kinkaid's Seventh Fleet, in particular the escort carriers, was closely involved in the landings.

The first Japanese force under Vice Admiral Kurita was extremely strong, but had no aircraft carriers with it. It *did* have two giant battleships, the *Yamato* and the *Musashi*, three other battleships, ten heavy cruisers, two light cruisers acting as destroyer leaders, and fifteen destroyers. The Japanese southern force, under Vice Admiral Nishimura, had another two battleships, a heavy cruiser and four destroyers. The second striking force, under Vice Admiral Shima, added three cruisers and another six destroyers. The Japanese aircraft-carrier force, under Vice Admiral Ozawa, was coming down from the north with four aircraft carriers, two converted carrier/battleships, three more

cruisers and eight destroyers and destroyer escorts. There were also transport groups and supply forces. In addition there were submarines, both American and Japanese, everywhere.

First reports that the Japanese were on the move came from the submarines USS *Darter* and USS *Dace*, operating together. After sending off a sighting report, the *Darter* duly sank the cruiser *Atago*, and the *Dace* sank the *Maya*. The *Darter* torpedoed another cruiser, but ran onto a reef and was lost – though her crew were rescued by the *Dace*.

As a result of the submarines' report, Admiral Halsey brought up three of his task groups, a total of eleven carriers, five fleet and six light fleet. The fourth of his carrier task groups was attacked by Japanese planes, and the USS *Princeton* was hit and had to be abandoned. The cruiser USS *Birmingham* was also badly damaged by explosions whilst trying to help the aircraft carrier.

The Battle of the Sibuyan Sea began on 24 October when four waves of American carrier aircraft attacked the Japanese Centre Force. This was a straightforward carrier-versus-battleship battle, in which the Japanese came off badly. The *Musashi* was sunk after suffering

some ten bomb and six torpedo hits. Most of the other battleships were hit, but none of them were put out of action. Kurita withdrew west.

The Battle of Surigao Strait began when the two other Japanese forces came in from the south, and plans were made to intercept them. Initially thirteen groups of three PT-boats each tried to interrupt their passage, and one Japanese cruiser, the *Abukuma*, was torpedoed. A series of torpedo attacks by destroyers followed, and these proved even more successful than the PT-boats. Torpedo hits were scored on the battleship *Fuso*, which later sank, together with three Japanese destroyers

What distinguished this battle from the others was that it was the last time battleships fought in classic line-of-battle style. It also demonstrated that centimetric radar now allowed those U.S. battleships equipped with it to fight a night engagement, and to do so at ranges that had never even been contemplated before.

As the remnants of Nishimura's striking force made its way up the Surigao Strait, Admiral Kinkaid gave Rear Admiral Oldendorf the order to deploy the six battleships, the *Mississippi*, the *Maryland*, the *West Virginia*, the *Tennessee*, the *California* and the *Pennsylvania*, so that they could prevent the Japanese reaching the Leyte landings.

Protected by both a left- and a right-flank cruiser squadron, this would have been a formidable force for Nishimura to tackle with just one battleship, a cruiser and a single surviving destroyer, even if he had been expecting reinforcement from the cruisers and destroyers of the second striking force coming up behind.

So indeed it proved. First the cruisers, and then the three battleships with centimetric radar opened fire, the *West Virginia* firing her first salvo at 22,800 yards. Between them the *West Virginia*, the *Tennessee* and the *California* fired over two hundred large-calibre armour-piercing shells. Nishimura's flagship, the battleship Yamashiro took a terrible hammering, as did the heavy cruiser *Mogami*. Ablaze, the *Yamashiro*, turned away, only to be torpedoed by the destroyer USS *Smoot*. She sank in about eight minutes, taking Admiral

The USS *Princetown* (left), a 10,000-ton light carrier, which was lost in a battle in central Philippine waters in November 1944. Her captain, 133 other officers and 1,227 of her crew were rescued.

Top right: an aerial view of landing craft at a more open beach at Leyte. In all, some 783 ships were involved in getting the massive assault force ashore.

Bottom right: a Japanese destroyer is shattered by bombs dropped from planes of the Far East Forces 38th Bomb Group. American air supperiority in most operations at this stage of the War ensured that the enemy had great difficulty in obtaining reinforcements and supplies.

Nishimura and most of her crew down with her.

The second Japanese striking force, under Vice Admiral Shima, and consisting of three cruisers and seven destroyers, still intended coming to support Admiral Nishimura's force. However, there was virtually nothing left of it. The destroyer *Shigure* and the completely disabled cruiser *Mogami* were all that remained. In fact, in her eagerness, Shima's flagship cruiser, the *Nachi*, collided with *Mogami*, thereby greatly reducing her speed. The cruiser *Abukuma*, torpedoed by PT-137, would be finished off the following day by land-based U.S.AAF planes. Admiral Shima finally withdrew his much depleted force of two cruisers and four destroyers. The two-stage Battle of the Surigao Strait was over.

The Battle of Samar was very nearly an American disaster. But for some luck, and some excellent ship handling by Rear Admiral Clifton Sprague, the Battles of the Leyte Gulf might have had a different significance for us today.

The main problem was that the split command between Admiral Halsey and Vice Admiral Kinkaid had resulted in neither guarding the San Bernardino Strait against Vice Admiral Kurita's first striking force. Halsey had been told that his primary task was the destruction of the major portion of the enemy fleet, and assumed this took precedence over supporting the Seventh Fleet at Leyte.

The portion of the enemy fleet Halsey set out to destroy was the Japanese carrier force to the north, and not the still very strong surface fleet of battleships and cruisers now heading for Leyte. In a sense, Halsey fell for the very lure that Admiral Toyoda, directing the overall Japanese strategy from afar, had intended.

Halsey also thought that the first Japanese striking force had been considerably weakened by the previous day's fighting. Exaggerated air reports had claimed at least four of its battleships as 'torpedoed and bombed', with one sunk, and heavy cruiser losses.

Certainly the 70,000-ton *Musashi* had gone down, but most of the force was intact and heading through the San Barnardino Strait, which each of the two American admirals thought the other was covering. Neither was, and so the Japanese striking force headed straight for the landing area, protected only by the three task force groupings of six escort carriers each. These were slow moving, lightly armed and almost unarmoured, and were never intended for fighting a fleet action.

The three groups, nicknamed Taffy One, Two and Three from their official nomenclatures TG 77.4.1, TG 77.4.2 and TG 77.4.3, were ranged in this numerical order, from south to north. Thus it was Rear Admiral Clifton Sprague's northerly Task Force, Taffy Three, that suffered the main brunt of Kurita's attack.

One of his planes spotted the Japanese bearing down like a wolf on the fold. At 0638 hours on 25th October the 18-inch guns of the *Yamato* opened up at 37,000 yards. By this time Admiral Clifton Sprague had organised his small carrier fleet into an almost wagon-train-like circle. He got his planes airborne and called desperately for help to his fellow

A final novelty in this battle that so often verged on disaster was the use of kamikaze bombers. These scored hits on several escort carriers: the *Santee* and the *Suwanee* from Taffy One, and the *Kitkun Bay*, the *Kalinin Bay* and the *St. Lo*, from Taffy Three. The escort carriers proved to be tough little ships, and most managed both to keep going and to continue operating aircraft, although the kamikaze bomber that went through the *St. Lo's* flight deck caused explosions in her hangar below, and thus sank her.

Off Samar the Americans lost two escort carriers, two destroyers and a destroyer escort. The Japanese lost three 8-inch gun cruisers. Both sides had several ships damaged. It was an unlikely victory; a fleet of escort carriers and their destroyers had caused a main battleship and cruiser fleet to withdraw.

The final battle, that of Cape Engano on 25 October, 1944, was won by the biggest battalion in keeping with the more usual Pacific tradition. The Japanese *did* achieve their purpose in luring Halsey away, but, with his blood up, he saw to it that their success cost them dearly.

Cape Engano was also a fairly one-sided battle, as by then the four Japanese aircraft carriers and two converted battleship/carriers were almost denuded of planes. Many of these had been forced to land ashore after flying to the limit of their range without finding targets. This left about seventy-six planes at the disposal of the Japanese. Halsey's combined aircraft force was ten times greater.

When Halsey's planes found Vice Admiral Ozawa's ships, the results were fairly conclusive. Four aircraft carriers, including the Pearl Harbor veteran *Zuikaku* were sunk. The other casualties were the lighter fleet carriers *Chitose*, *Chiyoda* and *Zuiho*. The two converted battleship/carriers escaped, as did the cruisers and all but one destroyer. The cruiser *Tama* had been damaged, however, and was later sunk by the submarine USS *Jallao*. *Jallao* was one of a five-submarine patrol waiting across the path of Admiral Ozawa's withdrawal.

Fighting would continue around Leyte for several more weeks, and kamikaze attacks would claim several more American lives. However, there is no doubt that the Americans eventually emerged victorious from all the very varied naval engagements that group together to form the Battles of the Leyte Gulf.

Left: the USS *Princetown*, hit amidships by Japanese bombs, burns fiercely. Eventually she had to be abandoned and was sunk by other U.S. warships.

Top right: U.S. Carrier Division 25 undergoing a two-and-a-half hour attack by Japanese forces off the Leyte Gulf. The photograph was taken from the USS *White Plains*.

Bottom right: the wakes of Japanese ships under attack in Tables Strait during the Battle of Leyte Gulf show the evasive action taken during a bombing attack.

commanders, Rear Admirals Felix Stump and Thomas Sprague. They too launched their planes, but were respectively sixty and 130 miles away. Rear Admiral Oldendorf's battleships were three hours sailing away.

Just when it looked as though Taffy Three would be obliterated there was a sudden rain squall, which hid the American force for a vital half-hour. It was now that Admiral Kurita, who fought the battle extremely badly, made his first mistake. He assumed that all American aircraft carriers had speeds of around 30 knots, whereas the escort carriers only did about 18 knots, and ordered his ships into a top-speed 'general chase'.

A gallant destroyer attack caused the *Yamato* to turn away and saw two cruisers hit, one by torpedoes and one by bombs. Three of the attacking ships were lost along with the escort carrier *Gambier Bay*. Revenge came when aircraft from Taffy One sank the cruiser *Chokai*, and aircraft from Taffy Two sank the *Chikuma*.

Still convinced that the escort carriers could do 30 knots, the Japanese admiral called off his pursuing ships. Harrassed by further aircraft attacks, he then decided to withdraw back through the San Barnardino Strait.

THE ATOMIC AGE BEGINS

The fighting in the last six months of the Second World War was as intense and as deadly as any that had gone before. Whilst the fighting in Europe may not have reached the level of attrition seen at Stalingrad and before Moscow and Leningrad, the complexity of the Rhine crossing operation was unprecedented in terms of what it required in the way of men, modern equipment and timing.

It was also during these last six months that the Germans launched their ultimate weapon, the V2 rockets, against England. These alone accounted for the deaths of three thousand people, mostly in the London area. For their part, the Allies devastated Dresden with a bombing attack that produced a 'firestorm' and killed a massive 120,000 people.

As the War drew to a close in Europe, it began to look as though the war in the Pacific had bitter months, if not years, still to run. There was every indication that the Japanese would fight to the last in defence of their homeland. Indeed many had already done so in the fight to hold on first to Iwo Jima and then to Okinawa. Numerous suicidal bayonet charges had been launched on land and kamikaze attacks had been made from the air.

Reluctantly General MacArthur began to

Left: on 16 January, 1945, aircraft from Vice Admiral John S. McCain's Fast Carrier Task Force attack Japanese shipping in Hong Kong harbour.

Firefighters on the USS _Intrepid_ deal with dozens of small fires (right) caused by bombs from a kamikaze plane, which hit the carrier in the Philippines. About fifty crewmen were killed. These kamikaze suicide planes, which were flown straight into Allied ships as a guided missile, were a final, desperate Japanese weapon.

The Essex-type aircraft carrier USS *Franklin* was hit by two 500-pound bombs while operating only sixty miles from Japan. Top left: a river of burning gasolene flows down her sides. Despite the damage she made port safely.

Bottom left: a kamikaze aircraft that missed its target, a U.S. aircraft carrier. A twin-engined bomber, it was hit by anti-aircraft fire, and crashed into the sea.

prepare his plans for the invasion of Japan. He would go first for the southern island of Kyushu, planned for 1 November, 1945, to be followed by Honshu and the Tokyo plain sometime in March 1946. It was calculated that the Allies might have to accept up to a million casualties as they fought their way overland to Tokyo.

Meanwhile, the battleships of the U.S. Third Fleet were undertaking what turned out to be their final amphibious responsibilities. They were employed to protect the landing forces and to act as bombardment artillery in assaults on the two key islands along the invasion route to Japan, Iwo Jima and Okinawa. The pre-invasion bombardment of Iwo Jima from the sea was the heaviest ever carried out. It was also a much more accurate bombardment than any carried out previously. The Americans were hinting of what was to come.

Fighting on Iwo Jima lasted over a month, from 19 February to 25 March, 1945, and saw the deaths of nearly 6,000 U.S. marines, with another 17,000 wounded. Of the 21,000 Japanese on the island only 216 survived, the rest were killed.

While still sometimes able to fight the Americans to a standstill on their heavily fortified islands, the Japanese could no longer operate naval task forces as they had done in earlier days. Due to the almost complete domination of the sea by American submarines, the Japanese were now desperately short of fuel and were sending ships into action with orders to beach themselves once their fuel ran out and fight on as coastal guns and forts.

While Allied battleships bombarded Japanese positions on shore, the long-range artillery of their carrier-borne aircraft attacked targets on both land and sea. There were also many U.S.AAF aircraft well placed on nearby islands, and very much involved in both the island battles and in attacking Japan itself.

The 64,000-ton Japanese battleship *Yamato* was sunk on 7 April, 1945, while heading for Okinawa. She was Japan's largest and most powerful surviving warship. she and her sister ship, the *Mushashi*, which had been sunk in the Battle of the Sibuyan Sea, were built in defiance of every single naval treaty limiting size and fire power. They had been thought almost unsinkable. Their nine 18-inch guns could fire shells thirty miles, each gun turret weighing as much as a small destroyer.

The *Yamato* sank after being hit by numerous bombs and a dozen torpedoes. From a total of 3,292 men on board, only 269 were rescued. This was the largest loss of life aboard a warship in history.

The day before the *Yamato* was sunk, the Japanese attacked the Okinawa invasion fleet with 340 bombers and 350 kamikaze planes. During the course of the fighting on Okinawa, which began with the landings on 1 April, 1945, the U.S. Navy lost thirty-six ships and had over 300 other vessels and landing craft damaged.

Nevertheless, by 19 April, 1945, the Americans had some 160,000 men ashore, and were making steady progress. Fierce fighting continued for the rest of April and throughout May, only coming to an end on 20 June, 1945, with the surrender of the island's civilian population.

The Japanese commander committed suicide, and his men, more than 100,000 of them, died defending the island. Only a few hundred survived, taking to the hills and caves. U.S. casualties incurred whilst capturing the island totalled 47,000 dead or wounded.

The Allied fleet under Admiral William F. 'Bull' Halsey was by now the greatest naval force ever assembled. It consisted of no less than nine fleet aircraft carriers, six light carriers, seven battleships, fifteen cruisers and sixty destroyers.

The British Pacific Fleet, about a quarter of this size, simply served as a task force under Halsey's command. British objectives were therefore entirely subordinate to the overall American strategy. The British contribution consisted of the battleship HMS *King George V*, three aircraft carriers, six cruisers and fifteen destroyers. Other ships were preparing to come out following the end of war in Europe, but forthcoming events would make this unnecessary. Those that did arrive were used for the relief and rescue of former prisoners of war and in the occupation of recovered Commonwealth and other territories.

One of the greatest strengths of the American fleet was its ability to refuel at sea, and then return to the attack within a day or so. The fleet had developed this necessary skill over three years of naval warfare in the Pacific. The practice was mainly new to the British, who often required twice as long to refuel from their own fleet train.

In July and August the U.S. Third Fleet was set

Left: firefighters busy clearing the debris of a kamikaze plane that had crashed onto a British aircraft carrier. As the most modern British carriers had specially reinforced steel flight decks, they generally suffered less from this kind of attack than the American carriers.

Right: all available space is taken aboard the USS *Missouri* to witness the signing of the Japanese surrender document on 1 September, 1945.

the task of breaking Japan's remaining defensive forces. They were to attack strategic targets on the Japanese mainland, and prepare the way for invasion in every way, from minesweeping to reconnaisance. This fleet was also given the task of obliterating the last surviving remnants of the Japanese Imperial Fleet, and of establishing control of the waters around Japan.

This it proceeded to do by bombardment and carrier strikes. On 14 July, 1945, the first bombardment of the Japanese mainland from the sea occurred, with the shelling of the coastal city of Kamaishi in northern Honshu. It was followed by attacks on iron and steel works at Muroran on the island of Hokkaido, even further north.

On 17 July, the British Pacific Fleet, operating with the U.S. Third Fleet, made its first raids on mainland Japan, attacking airfields and shipping north of Tokyo. Targets there included the airfields at Sendai, Masuda and Matsushita, and, on the west coast, the port of Niigata. HMS *King George V* was also included in Halsey's bombardment force shelling Hitachi and Mito. This constituted another first, a combined Allied bombardment of Japanese mainland targets.

It is perhaps fair to say that the naval bombardment was not particularly effective in terms of the number of targets hit. In terms of morale, however, it was a great success. Japanese civilians, by now used to air attacks, since much of Tokyo and Yokohama had by then been destroyed by B.29 Superfortresses, did not like this new form of attack, and retreated inland. Later, when land-based American bombers hit these industrial areas, many fire fighters were absent, thus increasing the fire damage from bombing.

Although it was summer, bad weather also hindered the Allied attacks from the sea. Carrier strikes often had to be called off due to heavy rain and poor visibility, and there were at least two typhoons that caused quite serious damage to American ships.

The next major event was an attack on the Japanese naval base at Yokosuka. Understandably, the Americans monopolised this action as a direct revenge for Pearl Harbor. The Japanese base was heavily defended, and the ships were tied up alongside the quays and protected from torpedo attacks. Nevertheless, the 38,000-ton battleship *Nagato* was very badly damaged by bombs, though

Right: the Japanese delegation arrives aboard the USS Missouri.

Left: General MacArthur signs the Japanese surrender documents.

technically she remained afloat. Twelve U.S. aircraft were lost.

A week later, on 24 July, 1945, the Americans took further revenge for Pearl Harbor. Some of the surviving ships of the Japanese Imperial Fleet were now lying at the naval base of Kure, situated by the so-called Inland Sea between the islands of Kyushu and Shikoku and mainland Honshu. These ships were no longer seagoing because of the fuel shortage, but they were still a powerful force when acting as defensive gun emplacements.

Again, the Japanese ships were protected from torpedoes. This time though the Americans had more success to sinking the battleship *Hyuga*, the aircraft carrier *Amagi*, and the cruiser *Tone*. All these attacks coming from the sea were coordinated with massive B.29 bomber raids from the Marianas.

It could only be a matter of time before the

Japanese navy ceased to exist. This finally came on 28 July 1945, when the Third Fleet made their concluding attack. Many ships were sunk or damaged, including two more Japanese battleships, the *Ise* and the *Haruna*, and a heavy cruiser. Once again the Americans reserved this task for themselves; Pearl Harbor had been remembered, and avenged in full at last.

On the night of 29 July the heavy cruiser USS *Indianapolis*, whilst on her way to Leyte, was torpedoed by the Japanese submarine I.58. She sank so quickly that she had no time to send out an S.O.S.. It was only by chance that survivors were spotted in the water a long time afterwards by a reconnaisance aircraft. Only 300 of her crew of 1,200 were rescued. The *Indianapolis* was the last major Allied warship to be sunk in the Second World War.

The heavy cruiser had just delivered to the island of Tinian a package containing some of the final parts needed for arming atomic bombs. The Japanese were then given one final chance to surrender and warned that if they did not do so 'utter destruction would follow'.

Admiral Halsey and his fleet were ordered to leave the area because a special operation was about to take place.

On 6 August, 1945, the first atomic bomb ever to be used in war was dropped on Hiroshima from the long-range B.29 bomber *Enola Gay*, piloted by Colonel Paul Tibbets. The bomb itself, code-named LITTLE BOY, contained a quantity of fissionable Uranium 235 material at one end and a trigger detonator of the same material at the other. When the detonator was activated 2,000 feet over Hiroshima, the smaller quantity of radioactive uranium hit the larger, the whole mass became critical and a huge explosion occurred that destroyed or damaged some eighty percent of Hiroshima. The familiar mushroom cloud followed.

Some 92,000 people died in the blast at Hiroshima. Another 60,000 suffered terrible injuries and radiation, and many of them would also die in the succeeding months and years.

On 9 August, 1945, the Russians declared war on Japan, and the United States dropped a second atomic bomb, this time on Nagasaki. This weapon, code-named FAT BOY, had plutonium as its fissionable material and used an implosion method for its detonation. When it was dropped, the plutonium collapsed into a critical mass to create a nuclear blast. This blast was even greater than the first, but caused marginally less damage and about a third fewer casualties than at Hiroshima, because Nagasaki was situated in much hillier countryside than Hiroshima.

On 12 August, 1945, the Japanese surrendered. It only remained to sign the peace treaty, which was done on 12 September, 1945, aboard Nimitz's flagship, the USS *Missouri*, in Tokyo Bay.

The atomic age had begun. It was clear that any future battle at sea between major world powers could never be quite the same.

Left: the British commander in chief, Admiral Lord Louis Mountbatten, talks to crewmen on the aircraft carrier HMS *Illustrious*. Although the war in the Pacific was primarily an American one, a British Far East fleet joined in the later stages, as soon as the war in Europe was over. British aircraft carriers attacked airfields and battleships bombarded Japan.

The war is over now and a cocky little American destroyer ties up alongside the shattered 17-inch gun Japanese battleship *Nagato* (top right) in the vast naval base at Yokosuka.

Bottom right: Admiral Halsey's majestic Third Fleet carries out Operation Snapshot, in which the whole force executed a simultaneous turn to starboard - just for the cameras.

BIBLIOGRAPHY

GENERAL REFERENCE
British Vessels Lost At Sea – 1914-18 and 1939-45
Facsimile reprint of four HMSO publications
Patrick Stephens, Wellingborough, Northants
Two volumes (1976/1977); Single volume (1988)
ISBN 1-85260-134-5

J. ROHWER and G. HUMMELCHEN, *Chronology of the War at Sea 1939-1945,*
Ian Allan, Shepperton (1972) (English translation)
ISBN 7110-0227-0

The Register of the Victoria Cross
(1981)   ISBN 0-906324-03-3

The Register of the George Cross
This England Books, Cheltenham, Gloucs. (1985)
ISBN 0-906324-06-8

Reginald M. LESTER, *The Observer's Book of Weather*
Frederick Warne & Co., London and New York (1970)
ISBN 0-7232-0064-5

BATTLE OF THE RIVER PLATE
Geoffrey BENNETT, *Battle of the River Plate*
Ian Allan Ltd., London (1972)
ISBN 0-7110-0280

James HANLEY, *The Battle of the River Plate*
Picture Post Special

CONVOY
Richard HOUGH, *The Longest Battle, (The War at Sea 1939-1945)*
Pan Books Ltd., London (1986)
ISBN 0-330-30074-1

Edwin P. HOYT, *The U-Boat Wars*
Robert Hale, London (1984)
ISBN 0-7090-2369-3

MEDITERRANEAN
Donald MacINTYRE, *The Battle for the Mediterranean*
B.T. Batsford (1964), Pan Books (1970)
ISBN 0-330-02525-2

Peter SHANKLAND and Anthony HUNTER, *Malta Convoy*
Collins, London (1961, reprinted 1972)
ISBN 0-00-192327-7

SINKING THE BISMARCK
Ludovic KENNEDY, *Pursuit – The Sinking of the Bismarck*
Collins/Fontana (1974/1975)
ISBN 0-00-634014-8

Kenneth POOLMAN, *Ark Royal*
William Kimber & Co.Ltd., London (1956)
New English Books, London (1974) (Paperback)
ISBN 450-01803-2

Baron Burkard von Mullenheim-Rechberg, *Battleship Bismarck: A Survivor's Story*
Grafton Books, London, 1982 (Bodley Head 1981)
ISBN 0-583-13560-9

RADAR AND SPECIAL WEAPONS
Patrick BEESLEY, *Very Special Admiral* (The Life of Admiral J.H. Godfrey CB)
(Hamish Hamilton, 1980)
ISBN 0-241-10383-5

Peter FLEMING, *Operation Sea Lion*
Pan Books, London & Sydney (1975)
ISBN 0-330-24211-3

Major Arthur HOGBEN, *Designed to Kill* (Bomb Disposal from World War I to the Falklands)
Patrick Stephens, Wellingborough (1987)
ISBN 0-85059-865-6

PEARL HARBOR
John WINTON, *War In The Pacific – Pearl Harbor to Tokyo Bay*
Sidgwick & Jackson, London (1978)
ISBN 0-283-98459-7

BATTLE OF THE JAVA SEA
Captain Geoffrey BENNETT R.N., *Naval Battles of World War II*
B.T. Batsford, London & Sydney (1975)
ISBN 0-7134-2997-6

BATTLE OF THE CORAL SEA
Captain Geoffrey BENNETT R.N., *Naval Battles of World War II*
B.T. Batsford, London & Sydney (1975)
ISBN 0-7134-2997-6

Japanese Naval Vessels of World War Two
(As Seen by U.S. Naval Intelligence 1942-1944)
Arms and Armour Press (1987)
ISBN 0-85368-847-8

BATTLE OF MIDWAY
Gordon W. PRANGE, *Miracle at Midway*
McGraw Hill (1982) Penguin Books (1983)
ISBN 0-14-006814-7

Peter C. SMITH, *The Battle of Midway*
New English Library (1976)
ISBN 45-002930-1

CONVOY PQ17
Cajus BEKKER, *Hitler's Naval War*
English translation, Macdonald & Jane's (1974)
ISBN 0-356-04508-0

BATTLE OF THE BARENTS SEA
J.P.W. MALLALIEU, *Very Ordinary Seaman*
Victor Gollancz (1944), Panther Books (1956)
ISBN 0-586-00570-6

Dudley POPE, *73 North*
(Hardback) Weidenfeld & Nicolson, London (1958)
(Paperback) Pan Books, London and Sydney (1976)
ISBN 0-330-24441-8

SUBMARINES
Peter CREMER, *U-333 – The Story of a U-Boat Ace*
Bodley Head, London (1984)
ISBN 0-370-30545-0

John TERRAINE, *Business in Great Waters*
(The U-Boat Wars 1916-1945)
Leo Cooper, London (1989)
ISBN 0-85052-7600

NORTH AFRICA AND SICILY
Charlotte and Denis PLIMMER, *A Matter of Expediency* (The Jettison of Admiral Sir Dudley North)
Quartet Books, London (1978)
ISBN 0-7043-2169-6

BATTLE OF THE ATLANTIC
Norman L.R. FRANKS, *Conflict Over The Bay*
William Kimber, London (1986)
ISBN 0-7183-0602-3

Kenneth POOLMAN, *Focke-Wulf Condor – Scourge of the Atlantic*
MacDonald & Jane's, London (1978)
ISBN 0-354-01164-2

Henry REVELY, *The Convoy That Nearly Died – The Story of ONS154*
William Kimber, London (1979)
ISBN 0-7183-0406-3

D-DAY
Lt-Commander P.K. KEMP, *Victory At Sea*
White Lion Publishers (1976 edition)
ISBN 7274-0027-4

Peter C. SMITH, *Hold The Narrow Sea* (Naval Warfare in the English Channel 1939-1945)
Naval Institute Press, Annapolis (1984)
ISBN 0-87021-938-3

BATTLES OFF GUADALCANAL
J.D. LADD, *Assault from the Sea 1939-1945*
(The Craft, The Landings, The Men)
David & Charles; London and Vancouver (1976)
ISBN 0-7153-6937-7

BATTLE OF THE PHILIPPINE SEA
Ivor MATANLE, *World War II*
Colour Library Books, (1989)
ISBN 0-86283-684-0

BATTLES OF LEYTE GULF
J.ROHWER and G. HUMMELCHEN, *Chronology of the War at Sea 1939-1945*
Ian Allan, Shepperton (1972) (English translation)
ISBN 7110-0227-0

THE ATOMIC AGE BEGINS
John WINTON, *The Forgotten Fleet*
Douglas-Boyd Books, 1989 (Michael Joseph 1969)
ISBN 0-95144480-0-5